Jokes Men
Won't
Laugh At

Also by Tom Hobbes

JOKES WOMEN WON'T LAUGH AT

Jokes Men **Won't** Laugh At

Tom Hobbes

BERKLEY BOOKS, NEW YORK

JOKES MEN WON'T LAUGH AT

A Berkley Book / published by arrangement with
the author

PRINTING HISTORY
Berkley edition / June 2002

Copyright © 2002 by Tom Hobbes
Book design by Kristin del Rosario
Cover design by Pyrographx

Visit our website at
www.penguinputnam.com

ISBN: 0-425-18520-6

BERKLEY®
Berkley Books are published by The Berkley Publishing Group, a division of Penguin Putnam Inc., 375 Hudson Street, New York, New York 10014.
BERKLEY and the "B" design
are trademarks belonging to Penguin Putnam Inc.

PRINTED IN THE UNITED STATES OF AMERICA

10   9   8   7   6   5   4   3   2   1

Many thanks to all who contributed jokes, including Andy, Bill, Doc, Doug, Ho, Howard, Jeremy, Jimmy, Ken, Michael, Phil, Paul, Ratso, Roz, and everyone at Gates Restaurant.

Men. You gotta love having them around, if only to do the heavy lifting, mow the lawn, or change a lightbulb. (Well, sometimes they'll change a lightbulb. See page 159.) The downside is that they leave their clothes on the floor and dirty dishes in the sink, and left to their own devices, they'll never change the sheets on the bed. They also drink, stay out all night, belch, and fart—not to mention sleep with your best friend if they think they can get away with it.

But there is one thing you can do about men—you can laugh at them. That's why I've written this book. These jokes are guaranteed to make women laugh, but just don't show them to the men in your life. They *won't* laugh, although you don't have to worry about offending them. They won't get most of the jokes.

—TOM HOBBES

Q: HOW DOES A WOMAN'S G-SPOT DIFFER FROM A GOLF BALL?

A: A man will spend twenty minutes trying to find a golf ball.

A man walks into a liquor store and asks the proprietor for a case of beer, any kind except Bud. The owner says, "What's wrong with Budweiser—don't you like it? The man says, "I hate it. Last night I drank a whole case of Bud and blew chunks." The owner says, "If you drink a case of any beer, you're going to throw up."

"You don't understand," the man replies. "Chunks is my dog."

In the backwoods of Alabama, Mr. Johnson's wife went into labor in the middle of the night, and the doctor was called out to assist in the delivery.

To keep the nervous father-to-be busy, the doctor handed him a lantern and said, "Here, you hold this high so I can see what I'm doing." Soon, a baby boy was brought into the world.

"Whoa there, Scotty!" said the doctor. "Don't be in a rush to put the lantern down . . . I think there's yet another one to come." Sure enough, within minutes he had delivered another baby.

"No, no, don't be in a great hurry to be putting down that lantern, young man. It seems there's yet another one!" cried the doctor.

The new father scratched his head in bewilderment and asked the doctor, "Do ya think it's the light that's attractin' them?"

Q: WHY IS IT SO HARD TO FIND A MAN WHO IS SENSITIVE, CARING, AND EMOTIONALLY MATURE?

A: Because they all have boyfriends.

A boy was walking down the street when he noticed his grandpa sitting on the porch, in a rocking chair, with nothing on from the waist down. "Grandpa, what are you doing?" he exclaimed. The old man looked off in the distance and did not answer him. "Grandpa, what are you doing sitting out here with nothing on below the waist?" the boy asked again.

The old man slowly looked at him and said, "Well, last week I sat out here without a shirt, and I got a stiff neck. This is your grandma's idea."

Q: WHY DID THE MAN KEEP EMPTY BEER BOTTLES IN THE FRIDGE?

A: For people who didn't drink.

This farmer has about 200 hens, but no rooster, and the farmer wants chicks. So he goes down the road to the next farmer and asks if he has a rooster. The other farmer says, "Yeah, I've got a great rooster, named Randy. He'll service every hen you've got. No problem."

Well, Randy the rooster costs a lot of money, but the farmer decides he'll be worth it. The farmer takes Randy home and sets him down in the barnyard, giving the rooster a pep talk.

"Randy, I want you to pace yourself now. You've got a lot of chickens to service here and you cost me a lot of money and I'll need you to do a good job. So take your time and have some fun," the farmer says with a chuckle.

Randy seemed to understand, so the farmer points toward the henhouse and Randy takes off like a shot. *Wham!* He nails every hen several times each. The farmer is just shocked. Randy runs out of the henhouse and sees a flock of geese down by the lake. *Wham!* He gets all the geese. Randy's up in the pigpen. He's in with the cows. Randy is jumping on every animal the farmer owns.

The farmer is distraught, worried that his expensive rooster won't even last the day. Sure enough, the farmer goes to bed and wakes up the next day to find Randy lying, apparently dead as a doorknob, in the middle of the yard. Buzzards are circling overhead.

The farmer, saddened by the loss of such a productive animal, shakes his head and says, "Oh, Randy, I told you to pace yourself. I tried to get you to slow down. Now look what you've done to yourself!"

Randy opens one eye, nods toward the sky, and says, "Shhhhhh! They're getting closer . . ."

🙰

Q: HOW CAN YOU TELL WHEN A MAN IS WELL HUNG?
A: When you can just barely slip your finger in between his neck and the noose.

🙰

Q: WHAT IS THAT INSENSITIVE BIT AT THE BASE OF THE PENIS CALLED?
A: The man.

An old geezer arrives to place a donation in a sperm bank. A nurse sends him to a room with a girlie magazine and a jar. Forty minutes later, she knocks on the door.

"I'm still not finished, ma'am."

"What's taking so long?"

"First I tried my left hand. Then I tried my right hand. But I just can't get the top off this jar."

Q: WHAT IS WEST VIRGINIA FOREPLAY?
A: "Sis, you awake?"

A widowed farmer hires a college student one summer to help around the farm. At the end of the summer the farmer says, "Son, since you have done such a fine job here this summer, I am going to throw a party for you."

The college guy says, "Great—thanks!"

So the farmer says, "Well, I hope you can handle a few beers because there will be lotsa drinkin' going on."

"Hey, I can drink just as much as anyone else, so I'll be just fine."

The farmer says, "There is also going to be a lot of fightin', so I hope you're ready."

The college kid says, "I've been working hard all summer and I think I'm in pretty good shape."

The farmer says, "Well, did I mention that there will be alotta sex?"

To which the college guy says, "Good. I've been out here all summer and I'm been dying for some action. What should I wear?"

The farmer says, "Oh, it don't matter. It's just going to be me and you."

🃏

Q: WHAT DO YOU CALL A MAN WITH 99 PERCENT OF HIS BRAINS MISSING?
A: Castrated.

🃏

A man in Iowa brought a mule to his farm, and within a week, the mule gave his wife a fatal kick to the head. The man's mother-in-law then moved to the farm to help care for the children, and within a month, the mule had killed her, too. At the older woman's funeral, the pastor was amazed to see the church packed to the doors. A crowd of men of all ages spilled out onto the front steps.

"Your mother-in-law must have been a much-loved woman," the preacher told the farmer.

"Oh, they're not here for her," the farmer explained. "They want to buy my mule."

🃏

After his annual checkup, Bob is shocked to learn that he has somehow contracted a rare disease and has only twelve hours to live. Arriving home in utter despair, he tells his wife the terrible news and begins to cry. Overcome with grief, Helen hugs him tight and says, "Honey, I'm going to give you a night you'll never forget!"

They go to bed early and make passionate love with an ardor they haven't felt in years. When they're done, Bob turns to his wife and says, "Honey, that was wonderful, the best 've ever had. Can we do it again?" This time it's even more passionate.

Later, as Helen is about to doze off, Bob gives her a nudge and says, "Honey, come on. How about one more time?"

"That's easy for you to say. *You* don't have to get up in the morning!"

Q: WHY DID GOD GIVE WOMEN NIPPLES?
A: To make suckers out of men.

A woman walks up to an old man sitting in a chair on his porch. "I couldn't help but notice how happy you look," she says. "What's your secret for a long, happy life?"

"I smoke three packs a day, drink a case of beer, eat fatty foods, and never exercise," he replies.

"Wow, that's amazing," she says, "How old are you?"

"Twenty-nine," he replies.

Two women are golfing. One says, "Oh, I just got a nice set of clubs for my husband."

The other says, "What a great trade!"

Diamonds are a girl's best friend. Man's best friend: a dog. Not too hard figuring out which sex is smarter.

Q: WHY WERE MEN GIVEN LARGER BRAINS THAN DOGS?

A: So they wouldn't hump women's legs at cocktail parties.

Two men drove to a deli for a sandwich because they heard about a contest there. When they went to pay, the men asked about the contest.

"If you win, you're entitled to free sex," said the cashier.

"How do we enter?" asked the first man.

"Well, I'm thinking of a number between one and ten. If you guess right, you win free sex."

"Okay, I guess seven," said the first man.

"Sorry, I was thinking of eight," replied the cashier. "Come back soon and try again."

The next week, the two men returned to the same deli for lunch. When they went inside to pay, the second man asked the cashier if the contest was still going on.

"Sure," replied the attendant. "I'm thinking of a number between one and ten. If you guess right, you win free sex."

"Two," said the second man

"Sorry, I was thinking of three," replied the cashier. "Come back soon and try again."

As they walked back to their car, the first man said to the second man, "You know, I'm beginning to think this contest is rigged."

"No way," said the second man. "My wife won twice last week."

A guy buys a Harley from a friend, who passes along some instructions for keeping it in tip-top shape. He says that before it rains, you have to rub Vaseline all over the bike. The new owner agrees to the regimen, then drives off to pick up his girlfriend, who is taking him to dinner at her parents' house for the first time that night.

On the way there, the girlfriend says, "Honey, we have this old tradition in our house. Whoever speaks first at the dinner table has to do the dishes. Do your best to keep quiet. Daddy will respect you for it."

At the dinner table, it's like a tomb. No sound is made. The family has obviously never seen someone as taciturn as this guy, and finally it annoys the girl's mother. She stands up, strips down, and throws herself in front of the guy. He doesn't say a word, but he does drop his pants and fuck her.

The silence continues until his girlfriend also strips down, hops on his lap, and he fucks her—all without making a sound.

Bored with the quiet, he stares out the window and notices gray clouds approaching. Thinking of his bike, he pulls out his jar of Vaseline.

"All right, damn it all," the father says, eyeing the Vaseline suspiciously. "I'll do the dishes."

A wife was complaining about her husband's spending all of his free time in a bar, so one night he took her along with him when he went out. "What'll you have?" he asked her.

"Oh, I don't know. The same as you I suppose," she replied.

So, the husband ordered a couple of shots of Jim Beam and threw his down in one swallow.

His wife watched him, then took a sip from her glass and immediately spat it out.

"Yuck, that's *terrible*!" she sputtered. "I don't know how you can drink this stuff!"

"Well, there you go," said the husband. "And you think I'm out enjoying myself every night!"

Fifty years from now, Kyle gets one of the first robot secretaries on the market. His friend Pete stops by to see the invention: a beautiful blonde that types 300 words a minute, speaks eight languages, and has a great rack.

"Is it okay if I take her into the conference room for a bit?" Pete asks.

"Sure," Kyle says.

Ten minutes later, Kyle hears dreadful screams coming from the conference room down the hall.

"Oh, shit," he says, "I'll bet I forgot to tell Pete her ass is a pencil sharpener!"

Q: HOW IS A MAN LIKE AN INFLAMED APPENDIX?
A: Both cause you extreme pain. Once they're removed, you realize you never really needed them.

Before leaving on his quest, King Arthur asks Merlin to create a magical chastity belt for Lady Guinevere, with a hole in the bottom. Whatever is stuck through the hole will be cut off by magical blades.

Three years later, Arthur returns and lines up the Knights of the Round Table. He has them all drop their trousers, and sure enough, each one is missing his cock, except for Sir Galahad.

"Sir Galahad," Arthur says, moved nearly beyond words. "You alone did not betray my trust. You alone were honorable enough to respect my love for m'lady. How can I repay such loyalty?"

But Sir Galahad couldn't speak.

Q: WHAT DO A CLITORIS, AN ANNIVERSARY, AND A TOILET ALL HAVE IN COMMON?

A: Men always miss them.

Two boys walk into a field with a lake in the middle. They see a naked woman swimming in it, and one immediately runs off.

The second boy runs after him, calling, "Why are you running away?"

The first boy replies, "My mom told me if I ever saw a woman without any clothes, I'd turn to stone. She must be right, 'cause when I saw that woman in the lake, my dick started!"

A guy comes home from work, walks into his bedroom, and finds a stranger fucking his wife. He says, "What the hell are you two doing?"

His wife turns to the stranger and says, "See. I told you he was stupid."

In a long line of people waiting for a bank teller, one guy suddenly started massaging the back of the person in front of him. Surprised, the man in front turned and snarled, "Just what the hell you are doing?"

"Well," said the guy, "you see, I'm a chiropractor, and I could see that you were tense. Sometimes I just can't help working."

"That's the stupidest thing I've ever heard!" the guy replied. "I'm a lawyer. Do you see me screwing the guy in front of me?"

When her late husband's will was read, a widow learned he had left the bulk of his fortune to his busty, twenty-five-year-old secretary. Enraged, the widow drove to the stone engraver's to change the inscription on her husband's tombstone.

"Sorry, lady," said the stonecutter. "I inscribed 'Rest in Peace' on your orders. I can't change it now."

"Very well," she said grimly. "Just add, 'Until We Meet Again.'"

One day a cowboy and a younger woman decide to get married. After a traditional wedding, they leave for their honeymoon. While they're driving down the road, the new bride sees two cows having sex.

She asks, "What are they doing?"

Her husband answers, "They're roping."

"I see," replies the bride.

After a few more hours of driving, they see two horses having sex. Again the bride asks, "What are they doing, honey?"

The husband answers, "They're roping."

She says, "Oh. I see."

Finally they arrive at their hotel. They wash up and start to get ready for bed. When they get into the bed, they start to explore each other's body. The bride discovers her husband's penis.

"What is that?" she says.

"That's my rope," he answers.

She slides his hand down a little farther and gasps, "What are those?"

"They are my knots," he answers.

Finally the couple begins to make love. After several minutes, the bride says: "Stop, honey. Wait a minute."

Her husband asks, "What's the matter, honey?"

The bride replies, "Undo those knots. I need more rope!"

Confucius say: Baseball no make sense. Man with four balls cannot walk.

A woman buys a mirror at a flea market and takes it home. One morning she looks at herself in it and jokingly chants, "Mirror, mirror, on my door. Make my bustline forty-four."

In a puff of smoke, her chest expands to a size 44.

Stunned, she tells her husband what happened.

He goes upstairs, drops his pants, and chants, "Mirror, mirror, on the door. Make my penis hit the floor."

Then his legs fall off.

A man driving down a narrow country road rounds a bend and finds a woman driving in a truck toward him.

"Pig!" she yells as they pass.

"Bitch!" he yells back as he makes the turn, and then slams into a 200-pound hog blocking the road.

Q: HOW IS MARRIAGE LIKE A HOT BATH?
A: Once you get used to it, it's not that hot anymore.

***

A sailor just off a ship walks into the only motel in town looking for a room.

"Sorry, son," the manager says. "Only space I got is a double vacancy with a guy already in it."

"That's fine," the sailor says.

"Had a guy leave in the middle of night from that room yesterday," says the manager. "Said he couldn't stand the snoring."

"I'll just be happy for a bed," the sailor says.

The next morning, the sailor bounces down the stairs, utterly refreshed.

"The snoring didn't keep you up?" the manager asks.

"Nope," the sailor says. "As soon as I got in bed, I kissed him on the lips and said, 'Good night, handsome.' He watched me all night long."

***

Three men at the pearly gates are met by Saint Peter, who tells them all is forgiven but he needs to query them about their lives. The answers will determine their mode of transportation in Heaven.

"How long were you married?" Saint Peter asks the first man.

"Twenty-seven years," he replies.

"And did you ever cheat on your wife?"

"Yes, eleven times."

"Not too good, my son. Here's your Topaz."

The next man had been married eleven years and cheated only once.

"You will drive a Volvo."

"Well, Saint Peter," the third man says, "I was married twenty-eight years and never cheated on my wife once."

"Very good, my son. Here is your Mercedes."

A week later, the Topaz and Volvo pull up to the sidewalk, where the third man is sitting, chin on his hands and a glum look on his face.

"What's the matter?" they ask.

"I just saw my wife up here riding a skateboard."

A couple is playing golf when the wife drives her ball into a mansion off the third green. They walk over to the house, find an open door, and discover the ball has crashed through a large window and knocked over an antique brass lamp. Sitting nearby on the couch is a large man dressed in silks.

"I am the all-powerful genie," he bellows. "I will grant each of you a wish."

The man says, "I want to be rich and famous."

The genie nods and says, "It shall be done."

The wife says, "I want to stay beautiful until I'm ninety-nine years old."

The genie nods again. "It shall be done."

Elated, the couple hugs, but the genie speaks again.

"There is a caveat," he says. "For these wishes to come true, I must sleep with the lady."

They look at each other and both nod yes. The genie has his way with the woman, then turns to her husband.

"How old is your wife?"

"She's thirty-three," the husband answers.

"Isn't that a little old to be believing in genies?"

Q: WHAT'S THE DUMBEST PART OF A MAN?

A: His penis. It has no brains, two nuts for best friends, and lives next to a real asshole.

✥

In a mental institution a nurse walks into a room and sees a patient acting like he's driving a car.

The nurse asks him, "Dan, what are you doing?"

Dan replies, "Driving to Chicago!" The nurse wishes him a good trip and leaves the room.

The next day the nurse enters Dan's room just as he stops driving his imaginary car and asks, "Well, Dan, how are you doing?"

Dan says, "I just got into Chicago."

"Great," replies the nurse. The nurse leaves Dan's room and goes across the hall into Kyle's room, and finds Kyle sitting on his bed furiously masturbating.

Shocked, she asks, "Kyle, what are you doing?"

Kyle says, "I'm screwing Dan's wife while he's in Chicago!"

✥

Q: WHAT HAS FOUR ARMS AND AN IQ OF 160?
A: Two guys watching a football game.

✥

"Last night I made love to my wife four times," the Parisian bragged, "and this morning she made me delicious crêpes and she told me how much she adored me."

"Ah, last night I made love to my wife six times," the Italian responded, "and this morning she made me a wonderful omelette and told me she could never love another man."

When the American remained silent, the Parisian smugly

asked, "And how many times did you make love to your wife last night?"

"Once," he replied.

"Only once?" the Italian snorted. "And what did she say to you this morning?"

"Don't stop."

🦊

Over breakfast one morning, a woman said to her husband, "I bet you don't know what day this is."

"Of course I do," he answered in a huff, going out the door to the office.

An hour later, the doorbell rang, and when the woman opened the door, she was handed a box containing a dozen long-stemmed red roses. At noon, a foil-wrapped, two-pound box of her favorite chocolates arrived. Later, a boutique delivered a designer dress.

The woman couldn't wait for her husband to come home.

"First the flowers, then the chocolates, and then the dress!" she exclaimed. "I've never had a more wonderful Flag Day in my life!"

🦊

Q: WHY DO THEY GIVE MEN IN NURSING HOMES VIAGRA?
A: So they won't roll out of bed.

🦊

Two little boys are sitting in the living room, watching TV with their parents. The mother looks over at the father, winks at him, and nods toward upstairs. The father understands, and they both get up and head toward the stairs.

The mother turns back to the two boys and says, "We're

going upstairs for a minute. You two stay here and watch TV. We'll be right back, okay?"

The two boys nod yes, and the parents take off upstairs. The elder of the two boys is old enough to know what's going on, and he gets up and tiptoes upstairs. At the top of the stairs, he peeks into his parents' room and shakes his head. He goes back downstairs to his little brother. "Come with me," he says.

The two little boys tiptoe up the stairs. Halfway up, the older brother turns to the younger and says, "Now remember, this is the same woman who used to bust our balls for sucking our thumbs."

※

David had been a faithful Christian and was in the hospital, near death. The family called their pastor to stand with them. As the pastor stood next to the bed, David's condition appeared to deteriorate and he motioned frantically for something to write on. The pastor lovingly handed him a pen and a piece of paper, and David used his last bit of energy to scribble a note, then he died. The pastor thought it best not to look at the note at that time, so he placed it in his jacket pocket.

At the funeral, as he was finishing the eulogy, he realized that he was wearing the same jacket that he had been wearing when David died. He said, "You know, David handed me a note just before he died. I haven't looked at it, but knowing David, I'm sure there's a word of inspiration there for us all."

He opened the note and read, "You asshole, you're standing on my oxygen tube!"

※

An elephant said to a naked man, "It's certainly cute. But can you pick up peanuts with it?"

17

A man sticks his head in a barbershop. "How long until I can get a haircut?"

The barber looks up from the lone chair in the shop and says, "About an hour."

The man doesn't come back until a week later, at the same time, and asks the same question. "About an hour," is the barber's answer.

A third week passes, and the man makes his third appearance in the shop. "About an hour," the barber says again. By now he's curious, so this time he asks his buddy to follow the guy to see what he's up to.

The friend is back in twenty minutes.

"So where does that guy keep going?" the barber asks.

"To your house."

Q: WHY ARE WOMEN SO BAD AT MATHEMATICS?
A: Because men keep telling them THIS much equals nine inches.

Q: HOW CAN YOU TELL WHEN A MAN HAS BEEN USING THE COMPUTER?
A: There's Wite-Out all over the screen.

An old man, Mr. Miller, lived in a nursing home. One day he went into the nurse's office and informed Nurse Jones that his penis had died.

Nurse Jones, realizing that Mr. Miller was old and forgetful, decided to play along with him. "It did? I'm sorry to hear that," she said.

Two days later, Mr. Miller was walking along the hall at the nursing home with his penis hanging outside his pants.

Nurse Jones saw him and said, "Mr. Miller, I thought you told me your penis had died."

"It did," he said. "Today is the viewing."

❦

Q: WHY DO MEN NAME THEIR PENISES?
A: Because they don't like the idea of having a stranger make 90 percent of their decisions.

❦

A jock walks into a drugstore and purchases a pack of condoms. "That will be $1.08, please," says the clerk.

"What's the eight cents for?" asks the jock. "It says one dollar right here on the packaging."

"Tax," replies the clerk.

"Gee," says the jock, "you usually just roll them on and they stay put!"

❦

Marge was in bed with the paperboy. All of a sudden, they heard a noise downstairs.

"Oh, my God, your husband is home! What am I going to do?"

"Just stay in bed with me. He's probably so drunk, he won't notice."

The fear of getting caught trying to escape was more powerful than the thought of getting caught in bed with Marge, so the young man stayed put.

Sure enough, Marge's husband came crawling into bed, and as he pulled the covers over him, he pulled the blankets, exposing six feet.

"Honey!" he yelled. "What the hell is going on? I see six feet at the end of the bed!"

"Dear, you're so drunk, you can't count. If you don't believe me, count them again."

The husband got out of bed, and counted. "One, two, three, four . . . By gosh, you're right, dear!"

<hr>

Jed and Craig were in an accident, and killed instantly. Upon Jed's arrival at the Pearly Gates, he is met by Saint Peter.

"Where is my friend Craig?" Jed asks.

Saint Peter replies, "Well, Craig was not as fortunate as you. He went in the other direction instead of getting into Heaven."

Jed is bothered by this and asks, "Well, could I see Craig one more time just to be sure he's okay?"

So, Jed and Saint Peter walk over to the edge of Heaven and look down. There is Craig, on a sandy beach, with a gorgeous sexy-looking blonde in a bikini next to him, along with a keg of beer.

"I don't mean to complain, but Craig seems to have it pretty nice down there in Hell," says Jed.

"It's not as it appears to be," says Saint Peter. "You see, the keg has a hole in it, and the blonde doesn't."

<hr>

One day a lady went into a confessional and said to the priest, "Father, I called a man a son of a bitch."

The father then replied, "What did he do to you?"

She recalled how she was walking down the street when a man walked up from behind and pinched her rear.

The priest interrupts, grabs her ass, and says, "Like this?"

She says, "Yes, just like that."

The priest replies, "Well, that is no reason to call him a son of a bitch."

So she continues with the story. "Then he grabbed my breast."

"Like this?" said the priest as he grabbed her breast.

"Yes, just like that."

"You still shouldn't have called him a son of a bitch."

She continues. "Then he stuck his penis in me."

"Like this?" replied the priest as he prodded her with his groin.

"Yes," she said. "Is what I said okay now?"

"No, that is still no reason to call him a son of a bitch," replied the priest.

At that point, she said, "Then he told me he had herpes."

The priest replied, "Why, that son of a bitch!"

An escaped convict broke into a house and tied up a young couple who had been sleeping in the bedroom. As he gagged the wife, the robber whispered something into her ear. As soon as he had a chance, the husband turned to his voluptuous young wife, bound up on the bed in a skimpy nightgown, and whispered, "Honey, this guy hasn't seen a woman in years. Just cooperate with anything he wants. If he wants to have sex with you, just go along with it and pretend you like it. Our lives depend on it."

"Dear," the wife hissed, spitting out her gag, "I'm so relieved you feel that way, because he just told me he thinks you have a really cute ass!"

St. Peter was guarding the gates of Heaven and decided he needed to cut down on admissions. He told the next three guys in line, "I'm only letting in the person who had the worst last day on Earth."

The first guy says, "Well, I found out my wife was cheating on me, so I rushed home to catch her in the act. When I got home, my apartment on the twenty-sixth floor was empty. But when I got out to the landing, I found a guy hanging there by his fingertips. I went and got a hammer and started pounding his fingers until he fell. He landed in some bushes, so he lived. I went and got the refrigerator and threw it down on him. But that was such a strain, I had a heart attack and died."

Saint Peter nodded, and asked for the second guy's story.

The second guy says, "Well, I was working out on the landing of my twenty-seventh-story apartment when I slipped and fell. I quickly caught myself on the next floor. So I thought I was going to be okay. Then this crazy guy came out and started pounding my fingers, so I had to let go. I thought it must have been my lucky day because I landed in some bushes and I lived. Then right as I got up, a refrigerator landed on me and here I am."

"Pretty bad," said Saint Peter, who nodded toward the next man.

The third man says, "Well, I was banging this woman when her husband came home. She hid me in the refrigerator, and that's the last thing I remember . . ."

A little boy and his grandfather are raking leaves in the yard. The little boy sees an earthworm trying to get back into its hole. He says, "Grandpa, I bet I can put that worm back in that hole."

The grandfather replies, "I'll bet you five dollars you can't. It's too wiggly and limp to put back in that little hole."

The little boy runs into the house and comes back out with a can of his grandmother's hair spray. He sprays the worm until it is straight and stiff as a board. The boy then proceeds to put the worm back into the hole. The grandfather hands the little boy five dollars, grabs the hair spray, and runs into the house.

Thirty minutes later, the grandfather comes back out and hands the boy another five dollars. The little boy says, "Grandpa, you already gave me five dollars."

The grandfather replies, "I know. That's from your grandma."

❧

Effective January 1, your penis will be taxed by the IRS according to size.

The brackets are as follows:

10–12 inches: Luxury Tax, $30.00

8–10 inches: Pole Tax, $25.00

5–8 inches: Privilege Tax, $15.00

4–5 inches: Nuisance Tax, $3.00

Males exceeding 12 inches must file under capital gains. Anyone under 4 inches is eligible for a refund.

Please do not ask for an extension!

❧

A minister, a priest, and a rabbi went for a hike one day. It was summer, and it was very hot outside.

They were sweating and exhausted when they came upon a small lake. Since it was fairly secluded, they took off all their clothes and jumped into the water.

Feeling refreshed, the trio decided to pick a few berries while enjoying their freedom. As they were crossing an open area, who should come along but a group of ladies from town.

Unable to get to their clothes in time, the minister and the priest covered their privates and the rabbi covered his face while they ran for cover.

After the ladies had left and the men got their clothes back on, the minister and the priest asked the rabbi why he covered his face rather than his privates.

The rabbi replied, "I don't know about you, but in my congregation, it's my face they would recognize."

Three old guys are sitting around complaining. The first guy says, "My hands shake so bad that when I shaved this morning, I almost cut my ear off."

The second guy says, "My hands shake so bad that when I ate breakfast today, I buttered half the table instead of my toast."

The third guy says, "My hands shake so bad that the last time I went to pee, I came just taking my cock out."

A circus owner runs an ad for a lion tamer, and two young people show up. One is a guy in his mid-twenties and the other is a gorgeous blonde about the same age.

The circus owner tells them, "I'm not going to sugarcoat it. This is one ferocious lion. He ate my last tamer, so you both better be good or you're dead. Here's your equipment: a chair, a whip, and a gun."

The woman says, "I'll go first." She walks past the chair, the whip, and the gun and steps right into the lion's cage. The lion starts to snarl and pant and begins to charge her, so she throws open her coat revealing her beautiful naked body.

The lion stops dead in his tracks, sheepishly crawls up to her, and starts licking her ankles. He continues to lick her calves, kisses them, and then rests his head at her feet.

The circus owner is stunned, and finally sputters, "I've never seen a display like that in my life." He then turns to the young man and asks, "Can you top that?"

"No problem," replies the young man. "Just get that lion out of the way."

<hr>

A fireman helping investigate a report of smoke from a sanitation plant fumbles through a service corridor and suddenly falls one story into a pool of raw sewage.

"Fire! Fire! Fire!" he yells while bobbing in the waste.

A crew of his fellow firemen burst through several doors only to be stopped in their tracks by the stench and the sight of their comrade.

"Why in the hell were you yelling 'fire'?" one of them asked angrily.

"Would you have come if I had yelled: 'Shit, shit, shit'?"

<hr>

Q: HOW MANY DIVORCED MEN DOES IT TAKE TO SCREW IN A LIGHTBULB?

A: Who knows? They never get the house.

An infamous stud walked into his neighborhood bar and ordered a drink. The bartender thought he looked worried and asked him if anything was wrong.

"I'm scared out of my mind," the guy replied. "Some pissed-off husband wrote to me and said he'd kill me if I didn't stop doing his wife."

"So stop," the barkeep said.

"I would," the womanizer replied, taking a long swill. "But the jerk didn't sign his name."

A man and his girlfriend are having a sexual encounter. He asks her to "go downtown," so, with a sigh, she gets on her knees in front of him and starts peering at his genitals, looking and tipping her head this way and that, studying the whole business.

After about five minutes of this, he asks her in a sort of an annoyed voice, "What are you doing?"

She replies, "I'm doing what I always do when I'm downtown with no money: just looking."

At the card shop, a woman was spending a long time looking at the cards, finally shaking her head no.

A clerk came over and said, "May I help you?"

"I don't know," said the woman. "Do you have any 'Sorry I laughed at the size of your dick' cards?"

Two old drunks are sitting in a bar. The first one says, "Ya know, when I was twenty and got a hard-on, I couldn't bend it with either of my hands. By the time I was thirty, I could bend it about ten degrees if I tried really hard. By the time I was fifty, I could bend it about twenty degrees, no problem. I'm gonna be sixty next week, and now I can almost bend it in half with just one hand."

"So," says the second drunk, "what's your point?"

"Well," says the first, "I'm just wondering how much stronger I'm gonna get!"

A fireman tells his bride that he wants sex when he comes home from the firehouse. "When I shout One Bell, it means get undressed. Two Bells, get in bed. Three Bells, spread your legs."

A few days later, he comes home to test his system.

"One Bell!" he yells, and his wife strips.

"Two Bells!" he yells, and his wife hops in bed.

"Three Bells!" he yells, and her legs part for him.

A few minutes into the lovemaking and suddenly his wife yells out, "Four Bells!"

"What the hell is Four Bells!?" the fireman snorts.

"It means I need more hose."

Woman: Most mornings I wake up grouchy. Sometimes, I let him sleep.

A jock grabbed a large thermos and hurried to a nearby coffee shop. He held up the thermos and the waitress quickly came over to take his order.

"Is this big enough to hold six cups of coffee?" he asked.

The waitress said it looked like about six cups to her.

"Oh, good!" he said in relief. "Then give me two regular, two black, and two decaf."

There was a boy playing in the farm field when his mom called him in for breakfast. On his way in he kicked a cow, pig, and a chicken. His mother watched this, then placed a bowl of dry cereal before him. "What's the deal?" he asked.

His mom says: "You kicked the cow, so no milk for you; you kicked the pig, so no bacon for you; and you kicked the chicken, so no eggs for you."

Then his father walked into the kitchen and accidentally kicked the cat.

The boy looked up at his mother and said, "Do you want me to tell him, or should you?"

A guy traveling through the prairies of Oklahoma stopped at a small town and went to a bar. He stood at the end of the bar, ordered a drink, and lit up a cigar. As he sipped his drink, he blew seven smoke rings in the air, one with each puff. Finally, an American Indian raced over to his bar stool, pointed his finger and said, "Now listen, buddy. If you don't stop calling me that I'll smash your face in!"

A young boy and his father were in a store when they walked past a rack of condoms. Being a curious boy, the youngster asked his father, "What are these things, Daddy?"

His dad said, "Condoms son."

The boy asked, "Why do they come in packs of one, three, and twelve?"

The dad replied, "The packs with one are for the high-school boys on Saturday night. The packs with three are for the college boys: Friday, Saturday and Sunday. And the ones with twelve of them are for married men: one for January, one for February, one for March . . ."

A man runs away and joins the French Foreign Legion, and he is stationed in a remote desert outpost. After a few weeks of loneliness, he approaches the commander. What do the men do about sex? he wants to know.

The commander points to a tent at the edge of camp. "There's a camel inside," he says.

The man grimaces and goes back to his barracks. But a week later, he can't stand it anymore. He goes to the tent and has sex with the camel.

On his way out, he passes the commander. "Thanks, Chief," he says. "That was a lot better than I thought it would be."

The commander looks puzzled. "You thought riding a camel to the brothel would be bad?"

Q: WHAT DID GOD SAY AFTER CREATING MAN?
A: I can do better.

There was a mother pregnant with triplets and one of the triplets asks the other two, "If you could be anything, what would it be?"

One of them answers, "I'd be a plumber so that I could get all of this water out of here."

Another says, "I would be an electrician so that we could have light in here."

The third triplet answers, "I'd be an exterminator so that I could kill that damn worm that keeps popping its head in here."

Two six-year-old boys were standing at the toilet to pee. One says, "Your thing doesn't have any skin on it!"

"I've been circumcised," the other replied.

"What's that mean?"

"It means they cut the skin off the end."

"How old were you when it was cut off?"

"My mom said I was two days old."

"Did it hurt?" the kid asked.

"You bet it hurt. I didn't walk for a year!"

Two twins enlisting in the army were getting their physicals. During the inspection, the doctor was surprised to discover that both of them possessed incredibly long penises. "How do you account for this?" he asked the brothers.

"It's hereditary, sir," the older one replied.

"I see," said the doctor, writing in his file. "Your father's the reason for your elongated penises?"

"No, sir, our mother."

"Your mother? But women don't have penises!"

"I know, sir," replied the recruit. "But she only had one arm, and when it came to getting us out of the bathtub, she had to manage as best she could."

A scuba diver is twenty feet below sea level when he sees another guy with no breathing apparatus or diving gear. He goes down another thirty feet, and the guy with no equipment stays with him. He takes out a waterproof chalkboard and writes, "How can you stay down this deep without equipment?"

The guy takes the chalkboard and writes, "I'm drowning, asshole."

◈◈

Q: WHAT IS THE DIFFERENCE BETWEEN A MAN AND A CATFISH?
A: One is a bottom-feeding scum-sucker with whiskers and the other is a fish.

◈◈

A couple were married, and following the wedding, the husband laid down some rules. "I'll be home when I want, if I want, and at what time I want," he insisted. "And I don't expect any trouble from you. Also, I expect a decent meal to be on the table every evening, unless I tell you otherwise. I'll go hunting, fishing, boozing, and card playing with my buddies whenever I want. Those are my rules," he said. "Any comments?"

His new bride replied, "No, that's fine with me. But just understand that there'll be sex here at seven o'clock every night . . . whether you're here or not."

◈◈

A woman came home just in time to find her husband in bed with another woman. With superhuman strength born of fury, she dragged her husband down the stairs to the garage and put his penis in a vise. She then secured it tightly and threw the metal handle through the window. Next she picked up a hacksaw. Terrified, her husband screamed, "Stop! Stop! You're not going to . . . to . . . cut it off, are you?"

The wife said, "Nope. You are. I'm going to set the garage on fire."

⚜

A golfer was on vacation in Ireland, and while playing he makes a hole in one. At that, a leprechaun jumps out from the trees and says, "I am the lucky leprechaun of the thirteenth hole, and I'll grant you a wish."

The player thought for a minute and said, "Could you make my dick a bit longer?"

Well, by the time he got to the fourteenth tee, it was showing below his shorts. He continued his game, and on the fifteenth hole, it was dragging along behind him. By the eighteenth, he could hardly make it to the green.

He went straight to the pro shop and asked the pro how to fix it. He was told that legend has it that you must go back and make another ace and see the leprechaun again. After purchasing five buckets of balls, the golfer made his way back to the thirteenth and frantically began hitting shot after shot until finally he made the hole in one. Again the leprechaun offered any wish.

Relieved, the player said, "Could you make my legs a bit longer?"

⚜

A father asked his ten-year-old son if he knows about the birds and the bees.

"I don't want to know!" the child said, bursting into tears.

Confused, the father asked his son what was wrong.

"Oh Dad," the boy sobbed. "At age six, I got the 'there's no Santa' speech. At age seven, I got the 'there's no Easter

Bunny' speech. Then at age eight, you hit me with the 'there's no Tooth Fairy' speech! If you're going to tell me now that grown-ups don't really have sex, I've got nothing left to live for!"

<hr>

A successful man is one who earns more money than his wife can spend. A successful woman is the one who marries him.

<hr>

An elderly man goes into confession and says to the priest, "Father, I'm eighty years old, married, have four kids and eleven grandchildren. I started taking this new Viagra pill, and last night I made love to two eighteen-year-old girls. Twice. Once with the both of them in the same bed."

The priest says, "Well, my son, when was the last time you were in the confessional?"

"Never, Father," the man says. "I'm Jewish."

"So then, why are you telling me?"

"Hell! I'm telling everybody!"

<hr>

Sign Number 45 that she is getting bored with sex:
    She cusses when the ashtray falls off his ass.

<hr>

Q: WHAT'S THE DIFFERENCE BETWEEN A MAN AND A TOILET?
A: A toilet won't follow you around after you've used it.

<hr>

Two guys from the sticks are on their first airplane ride. Midway through the flight to New York, a breathless pilot comes on the intercom. "Ladies and gentlemen, I am afraid we have lost one of our three engines. We are heading for Chicago right now."

The guys keep reading their comic books when, five minutes later, the pilot comes on again.

"I am afraid we have lost our second engine."

One guys turns to the other and says, "Boy, I hope we don't lose that third engine. We'll be up here all day."

An old man walks into a doctor's office and says, "I'd like you to give me something to lower my sex drive."

"Excuse me?" the doctor asks. "You're saying your sex drive is too high?"

"That's right," the man says. "It's all in my head, and I need it to be about three feet lower."

These two poor kids go to a birthday party at a rich kid's house. The kid is so rich that he has his own swimming pool, and all the kids go in. As they're changing afterward, one of the poor kids says to the other one, "Did you notice how small the rich kid's penis was?"

"Yeah," says his friend. "It's probably because he's got toys to play with."

An old couple celebrating their sixty-fifth wedding anniversary are flipping the cable TV channels when they come across some porn. The old man looks at the woman and says, "So, do you think we could do it like them?"

She says, "I don't see why not."

So he goes upstairs and takes a shower, puts on some aftershave, and tries to look nice for her. He comes back down to his wife, only to find her standing on her head.

"What the hell are you doing?" he asks.

"Well," she replies, "I thought if you couldn't get it up, maybe you could drop it in."

A little boy was out with his grandfather when they came across a couple of dogs mating on the sidewalk.

"Why are they doing that, Grandpa?" asked the little boy.

The Grandfather was embarrassed, so he said, "The dog on top has hurt his paw, and the one underneath is carrying him to the doctor."

"They're just like people, aren't they, Grandpa?" said the little one.

"How do you mean?" asked Grandpa.

"Offer someone a helping hand," said the little boy, "and he'll screw you every time!"

A man goes out to a bar and comes home a few hours later plastered.

"How dare you come home half drunk!" screams his wife.

"It's not all my fault," he replies. "I ran out of money."

A husband and his wife who have been married twenty years were doing some yard work. The man was working hard cleaning the barbecue grill while his wife was bending over, weeding the flower bed. The man says to his wife, "Your rear end is almost as wide as this grill." She continues gardening and ignores the remark.

A little later, the husband takes his measuring tape and measures the grill, then he goes over to his wife while she is bending over, measures her rear end, and gasps, "Jeez, it really IS as wide as the grill!" She ignores this remark as well.

Later that night while in bed, her husband starts to feel frisky. The wife calmly responds, "If you think I'm gonna fire up the grill for one little wiener, you're mistaken."

One day, a regular at a bar who is usually a very light drinker goes into the bar looking very sad. He orders a double Scotch and downs it one gulp.

"What's wrong?" the bartender asks. "Got troubles?"

The man replies, "I just came home early from work and found my wife in bed with my best friend. I told her to pack her bags and go; it's finished between us."

The bartender says, "What about your friend?"

The man says, "I looked him straight in the eye and said, 'BAD DOG!'"

An obnoxious man meets a woman in a bar and says to her, without any small talk beforehand, "I'd really like to get into your pants."

"No thanks," she says. "There's already one asshole in there."

Bombed, an old man turned to the woman next to him in a bar and said, "How about you and me, honey?" The woman looked him up and down, then picked up her purse to move three stools away.

Ticked, the man shouted after her, "You sure look like you could use the money, but I don't have three dollars!"

She looked up and said, "Who says I charge by the inch?"

A farmer is lying in bed with his wife when he turns to her grabs her tits and says, "Honey, if you could get milk out of these, we could sell the cow." Then he grabs between her legs and says, "Honey if you could get eggs out of here, we could sell the chickens."

She turns to him, smiles, grabs his dick, and says, "Honey if you could get this up, I could get rid of your cousin."

A young man has a nervous tick that causes him to wink one eye uncontrollably. But aspirin usually weakens the action. He goes into a job interview, which is going very well, but then feels the aspirin beginning to wear off. He starts winking uncontrollably, which begins to rattle the interviewer.

"Sir, is there a problem?" the interviewer asks.

"No, I'm sorry. It's just that sometimes I can't stop winking. Usually aspirin takes care of it . . ."

He reaches inside to grab his pills, and out fall six condoms.

"Sir!" the interviewer says. "We can't have a womanizer working for us!"

"No, no, you don't understand," the man says. "Have you ever walked into a pharmacy winking and asking for aspirin?"

A guy and an alien are sitting at a bar. The alien keeps poking the guy's cheek with his finger and going, "Dzzzt."

Finally the guy says, "If you do that one more time, I'm going to chop your dick off."

But the alien does it again, so the guys rips off the alien's pants. Stunned, he finds nothing there.

"Huh," the guy says. "So how do you have sex?"

The alien pokes him with his finger and goes, "Dzzzt."

This guy has a crush on a girl at work. He is dying to ask her out on a date, but every time he sees her, he gets the biggest erection ever. There is nothing he can do to control it.

After some time, he decides to get her phone number and call her up. That way, he won't have to see her and he won't get too excited. He ends up asking her out and she says yes.

He figures what he'll do is tie his manhood to his leg so when he sees her it won't make a bulge in his pants and she'll never notice it.

On the night of their date, he goes to her house. When he rings the bell, she answers the door wearing nothing but a smile.

And he kicks her in the face.

During a lull in the wedding rehearsal, the groom and best man, two longtime friends, began to compare conquests. Each is proud of his skills as a swordsman.

Looking out over the crowd, the groom says, "You know, Bill, except for my wife-to-be, my two sisters, and my mother, I've been to bed with every woman in this room."

To which his friend responds, "Well then, between the two of us we've had them all!"

※

Husband: Put your coat on, my love, I'm going to a bar.
Wife: Are you taking me out for a drink?
Husband: Don't be silly, woman, I'm turning the heat off while I'm out.

※

Q: WHY ARE MEN LIKE BLENDERS?
A: Every woman has one, and doesn't know why!

※

"Doc, I think my son has VD," a patient told his urologist on the phone. "And he got it from our maid."

"Okay, don't be hard on him. He's just a kid," the medic soothed. "Get him in here right away and I'll take care of him."

"But, Doc. I've been screwing the maid, too, and I've got the same symptoms he has."

"Then you come in with him and I'll fix you both up."

"Well," the man admitted, " I think my wife has it, too."

"Son of a bitch!" the physician said. "That means we've all got it!"

※

Husbands are like children. They're cute, as long as they belong to someone else.

※

Two young men go into a church to confess their sins. The first one steps into the confessional and sits down.

He says, "Bless me, Father, for I have sinned. I have had premarital sex."

"Who was it with, my son? Was it one of the women in the congregation?"

"I am sorry, Father, I cannot divulge the woman's name. It would ruin her reputation."

"Well, tell me, was it Sarah-Lou?"

"No, Father."

"Was it Peggy-Sue?"

"No, Father. I cannot tell you. If I told the woman's name to anyone, her reputation would follow her everywhere."

"Was it Sally-May?"

"I am sorry, Father, I just can't say."

"Well then. Repeat four Hail Marys and five Our Fathers, and go and sin no more."

As the young man leaves the confessional, the second one grabs him. "So what did he give you?"

"Four Hail Marys, five Our Fathers, and three good leads."

Two guys are standing in front of the urinals in a men's room when Frank looks down at Bob's cock.

"Good Lord, Bob, it's twisted like a pig's tail."

"Yeah," Bob says, "isn't yours?"

"No, it's straight."

Bob looks down. "Good God. I guess I've never looked at another guy's. Are they all like that?"

"Of course," Frank says, giving his a shake.

"Wait," Bob says. "You shake yours?"

"Of course I do."

"Ah, jeez," Bob says. "I've been wringing mine all these years."

Three guys walk in a strip bar and approach a woman dancing naked on the center stage. The first man licks a $100 bill and slaps it on one side of her butt. The next guy also licks a $100 bill and slaps it on the other side of her butt. The third guy walks in, takes out a credit card, swipes it through her butt, and takes the $200.

A grandfather sat his grandson down the night before his wedding.

"Son, sex changes. When you're first engaged, it's tri-weekly. Once you get married, though, it's try weekly. When you're my age, it's try weakly."

Mrs. Smith and Mr. Hurt, two longtime friends now living in the same nursing home, are sitting in the community room one day when the woman says, "If you kiss me once, John, I'll have sex with you on that rocking chair.

"If you kiss me twice, I'll have sex with you on the couch.

"And if you kiss me three times, I'll take you back to my room for a romantic evening."

John Hurt marches over, grabs Mrs. Smith by her shoulder, and kisses her three times.

"Oh John," she says, "you want a romantic evening."

"Nope," he says, "just three times on the rocker."

Q: WHY IS A BUFFET BETTER THAN A MAN?
A: Because you don't have to wait an hour for seconds.

The man told his doctor that he wasn't able to do all the things around the house that he did when he was a younger man. When the examination was complete, he said, "Now, Doc, I can take it. Tell me in plain English what is wrong with me."

"Well, in plain English," the doctor replied, "you're just lazy."

"Okay," said the man. "Now give me the medical term so I can tell my wife."

"Darling," the man asked his wife in the morning, "did you fake it last night?"

"No," she answered. "I really was asleep that time."

A guy goes out to a nightclub, meets a girl, and she invites him back to her place for the night. Her parents, who work a concession at a carnival, are out of town and this is the perfect opportunity to have company over. They get back to her house and go into her bedroom. When the guy walks in the door, he notices all these fluffy toys. There's hundreds of them—fluffy toys on top of the wardrobe, fluffy toys on the bookshelf and windowsill, fluffy toys on the floor, and of course fluffy toys all over the bed.

Later, after they've had sex, he turns to her and asks, "So, how was I?"

She says, "Well . . . you can take anything from the bottom shelf."

Late one night, a woman was walking home when a man grabbed her and dragged her into the bushes.

"Help me! Help me!" she screamed. "I'm being robbed!"

"You ain't being robbed!" her attacker interrupted. "You're being screwed!"

The woman looked down at her attacker as he unzipped his jeans. "If you're screwing me with that," she fumed, "I am being robbed!"

Q: WHY DID THE GOOSE GO TO THE BASKETBALL GAME?
A: Because he heard the referee was blowing too many fouls.

An elderly couple hear from their doctor that the wife has a severe heart problem. If she ever has sex again, the doctor says, she will die. The two decide to sleep apart, fearing the temptation would be too great if they sleep near each other. It works well for weeks, until they both find that they can't sleep at all out of the longing.

One night, they nearly collide on the stairs, the husband heading upstairs from the couch, the wife coming downstairs from the bedroom.

"Darling," the wife says, "I must confess. I was about to commit suicide."

"That's good," the husband says. "Because I was coming upstairs to kill you."

Earl spent most every night in a bar across town, getting drunk to the point that his vision became hopelessly blurred.

As a result, when he came home, he always fumbled with his house key for fifteen minutes, then staggered in to find his wife yelling at him and throwing pans at his head.

After reading an advice column, Earl's wife decided to change tacks and treat him kindly when he staggered in, thinking it might guilt him into doing right by her.

That night, as Earl fumbled with the key, his wife whipped open the door, greeted him with a strawberry dripping in chocolate, then kissed him softly on the cheek and invited him in.

"Would you like to go upstairs and make love to me, Earl?" she asked.

"Might as well," he said. "My wife is already pissed at me for being late."

On their wedding night, the young bride went up to her new husband.

"Since we're married now, I'm rearranging our sex life to suit my schedule. In the evening, if my hair is done, that means I don't want sex at all. If my hair is somewhat undone, that means I may or may not want you to take me. And if my hair is completely undone, that means I want sex."

"Okay, sweetie," the groom replied. "When I come home, I usually have a drink. If I have only one drink, that means I don't want sex. If I have two drinks, I may or may not want it. But if I have three drinks, I don't give a fuck about your hair."

A dog, a cat, and a penis are sitting around a campfire one night. The dog says, "My life sucks, my master makes me do my business on a fire hydrant!"

The cat says, "That's not so bad. My master makes me do my business in a box of dirt."

The outraged penis says, "At least your master doesn't put a bag over your head and make you do push-ups until you throw up!"

Q: ARE BIRTH-CONTROL PILLS TAX DEDUCTIBLE?
A: Only if they don't work.

Mrs. Haynes is having her house painted, and her husband comes home from work and leans against the freshly painted wall.

The next day, she says to the painter, "You wanna see where my husband put his hand last night?"

The painter sighs and says, "Look, lady, I got a tough day's work ahead of me. Why don't you just make us a cup of tea?"

A woman who's just acquired two female birds approaches her priest, who she knows keeps parrots.

"Father," she whispers, "I bought two parrots and they apparently once lived in a whorehouse. All they know how to say is, 'Get your blow jobs here.'"

"That's horrible," the priest says. "You must send them to me. My birds rub rosary beads with their beaks and quote Scripture."

A few days later, the woman drops off her two birds to spend the week with the priest's two male birds. As she puts the cage down, her two birds begin squawking. "Get your blow jobs here. *Squaaawwk!* Get your blow jobs here."

One of the priest's birds turns to the other: "Put your beads down. Our prayers have been answered."

🛡️

Superman was flying around Metropolis looking for trouble when he spotted Wonder Woman apparently sunbathing nude on top of a building. "Well," he thought to himself, "I'm so fast I bet I could fly down there and nail her before she even knew what hit her." So he undid his yellow belt, lowered his red shorts, flew down, did his thing, and soared off into the Metropolitan sky.

Wonder Woman lay stunned. "What was that?" she said out loud.

"I don't know," groaned the Invisible Man. "But my ass sure is sore now."

🛡️

Bob and Bill, two eighty-year-olds were discussing sex.

Bob said, "Bill, I hear they have a new drug out that helps you have sex, and I think it's called Viagra."

Bill said, "Can you get it over the counter?"

Bob thought for a minute and said, "Maybe if you take two or three."

🛡️

Q: HOW DO YOU KNOW WHEN A MAN IS ABOUT TO SAY SOMETHING INTELLIGENT?

A: He prefaces his words with: "The other day my wife told me that . . ."

🛡️

A rural couple had made sacrifices to save money to send their only son to college. Once there, he began to grow long sideburns, a mustache, and a goatee. When his facial hair was luxurious enough to satisfy him, he had his photograph taken and mailed it home with a note that read, "Fascinating, isn't it? Don't I look a bit like a count?"

"You idiot!" his father wrote back. "Here we are spending a fortune on your education and you can't even spell!"

🃏

At a big cocktail party, an obstetrician's wife noticed another guest, a big, oversexed woman, was making overtures to her husband. But it was a large, informal gathering, so she tried to laugh it off, until she saw them disappear into a bedroom together. She rushed into the room, found them in bed, and pulled the woman off the bed and onto the floor. "Look, lady! My husband just delivers babies, he doesn't INSTALL them!"

🃏

"Can you explain to me how this lipstick got on your collar?" the suspicious wife sneered.

"No, I can't," the husband replied. "I distinctly remember taking my shirt off."

🃏

An Alabama family took a vacation to New York City. For an adventure, the father took his son to see a skyscraper. They were amazed by everything they saw—especially the elevator at one end of the lobby.

The boy asked, "What's that there, Paw?"

The father responded, "Well, son, I reckon I never did see

nothing like this in my entire life. I got no derned idea what it is!"

While the boy and his father were watching in wide-eyed astonishment, an old lady in a wheelchair rolled up to the moving walls and pressed a button. The walls opened and the lady rolled between them into a small room. The walls closed and the boy and his father watched small circles of lights above the walls light up. They continued to watch the circles light up in the reverse direction. The walls opened again, and a voluptuous twenty-four-year-old woman stepped out.

The father turned to his son and said, "Go git your maw."

🝑

Impotence is Mother Nature's way of saying, "No hard feelings."

🝑

Two executives are getting ready to tee off for the fourth hole when another taps one of them on the shoulder and hands over a card. "Sir," it reads, "I am deaf and mute. May I play through?"

"ABSOLUTELY NOT!" one of the executives shouts at him. "Your disability does not in any way give you that privilege."

The pair continue with their game until, two holes later, one is nailed by a low drive that smacks him in the small of the neck. His partner twirls around to see the deaf mute with a three-wood in one hand. His other hand is lifted high, with four fingers in the air.

🝑

48

A woman goes to her doctor, complaining that her husband is 300 percent impotent.

The doctor says, "I'm not sure I understand what you mean."

She says, "Well, not only can he not get it up, but he's also burned his finger and his tongue."

A girl asks her boyfriend to come over Saturday night and have dinner with her parents. Since this is such a big event, the girl tells him that after dinner, she would like to have sex with him for the first time.

The boy is ecstatic, because he has never had sex before. He goes to the pharmacy to get some condoms, and the pharmacist helps the boy for about half an hour. He tells him everything there is to know about condoms and sex. At the register, the pharmacist asks the boy how many condoms he'd like to buy: a three-pack, ten-pack, or a family pack. The boy insists on the family pack because he thinks he will be rather busy, it being his first time and all.

That night, the boy shows up at the girls' parents' house and meets his girlfriend at the door. "Oh, I'm so excited for you to meet my parents! Come on in!"

The boy goes inside and is taken to the dinner table, where the girl's parents are seated. He freezes in his tracks, then turns to leave. The girl grabs him and whispers, "Where are you going?"

"Home," he whispers back. "Why didn't you tell me your father was a pharmacist?"

A guy is on a plane next to a woman. He sneezes, then takes his handkerchief and shoves it down his pants. The woman assumes he has a bladder problem, so she tries not to stare when he sneezes again and follows it with a plunge into his pants with the handkerchief.

When he does it a third time, he sees her staring and explains himself. "I actually have a very rare medical condition, in which a sneeze causes me to have an orgasm."

"Oh my," the woman says. "Do you take anything for it?"

"Yes," he answers. "Pepper."

A couple is going at it in the backseat of their car on a back-street when a cop raps on the window with his flashlight.

"Sorry, Officer," the guys says, pulling on his underwear. "Guess we got carried away."

"I'm still giving you a speeding ticket."

"Speeding ticket?" the girl asked.

"For doing sixty-nine in a thirty-five-mile-per-hour zone."

Q: WHY ISN'T A PENIS EVER OUT DRINKING LATE?
A: His best friends are all pussies.

Q: WHY DO MEN MASTURBATE SO MUCH?
A: So they can have sex with someone they love.

A man is talking to his doctor about a sexual problem.

"My wife wakes me up at 3:00 A.M. every day to make love, and we go for two hours and then I get up for work."

"Oh, I think I see the problem," the doctor says.

"No, that's not it. On the train in, there's this girl I meet in the bathroom, and we go at it for the hour it takes to get to the city."

"Ah, well—"

"Hold on, Doc. Once I get to work, my secretary is hot for me, and we usually fuck at least four times a day in my office."

"Oh my, perhaps—"

"I take a different train home, and there's another woman who goes down on me when we sit in the back row. Then my wife misses me so much, she usually throws me on the kitchen counter as soon as I walk in the door. Sometimes we miss dinner altogether."

"Well," the doctor says, "what exactly is your problem, then?"

"It hurts when I masturbate."

***

A man comes home from work and finds his wife admiring her breasts in the mirror. He asks, "What are you doing?"

She replies, "I went to the doctor today, and he told me I have the breasts of a twenty-five-year-old."

The husband says, "Well, what did he say about your fifty-year-old ass?"

She replies, "Actually, your name never came up."

***

Just think: If it weren't for marriage, men would go through life thinking they had no faults at all.

***

An army chaplain, walking through a notorious section of town, saw a soldier exiting a known house of prostitution. The soldier paused on the sidewalk and gestured with his right hand in a manner familiar to the good Catholic chaplain.

The chaplain promptly approached the wayward soldier, saying, "I'm sorry to see a good Catholic lad like you coming out of a place like that."

"Well, Father, actually I'm a Methodist," answered the soldier.

"But I clearly saw you cross yourself as you came out of there."

"When I come out of a place like that, I always check four things: my spectacles, my testicles, my watch, and my wallet."

⚜

"It's just too hot to wear clothes today," said Jack as he stepped out of the shower. "Honey, what do you think the neighbors would think if I mowed the lawn like this?"

"Probably that I married you for your money," she replied.

⚜

Women will never be equal to men until they can walk down the street with a bald head and a beer gut and still think they are beautiful.

⚜

Q: WHO FAKES MOST DURING SEX?
A: Men. (Sure, a woman can fake an orgasm. But only men can fake entire relationships.)

⚜

Stan and Jason have sold cars together for years. One day Stan says, "I love my wife, but sometimes I get bored. Tell me, have you ever thought of switching? Who says you have to be with your wife and I have to be with my wife all the time!"

Jason says, "Hey, that's a great idea. Let's talk to our wives and see what they think."

Each of them talks to his wife, and much to their delight, the wives agree to the plan.

The next morning Jason says to Stan, "How was it for you?"

Stan says, "I had a lot of fun, we should do this again."

"That's what I think," says Jason. "Let's go next door and see how the girls made out."

A guy calls in sick to work, and his boss asks, "How sick are you?"

"Well, I'm in bed with my sister."

Three countries decided to do scientific research on the penis: the United States, England, and Ireland. The United States invested $100,000 to research why the head of the penis is bigger than the shaft. After the research was completed, they concluded that it was for the pleasure of the woman.

The English thought that was wrong. So they invested $125,000 to research the same question: Why is the head of the penis bigger than the shaft? They concluded that it was for the pleasure of the man.

The Irish thought that both the English and the United States were wrong. So they put seventy-five dollars into re-

ning the same thing, and concluded that it was so that
hand will not hit you in the forehead.

❖

Q: WHAT DO WOMEN CALL A HANDCUFFED MAN?
A: Trustworthy.

❖

Q: WHY ARE GUYS SO SMART DURING SEX?
A: Because they're plugged into a genius.

❖

Q: HOW IS A VACUUM CLEANER LIKE A PORSCHE?
A: Both have dirt bags inside.

❖

An old man on his deathbed is talking to his wife.

"When I am gone I want you to marry George Kramer," he
begs her.

"Why George Kramer?" his wife asks. "You've hated him
all of your life!"

"I still do," gasps the old man.

❖

A large pharmacy with an ample supply of prescription drugs
was robbed. Two men entered the back of the store, but only
stole the store's entire supply of Viagra. The police are looking for a pair of hardened criminals.

❖

Jason rents an apartment in Chicago and goes to the lobby to put his name on the mailbox. While he is there, an attractive woman comes out of the apartment next to the mailboxes wearing a robe. Jason smiles at her, so she strikes up a conversation with him. As they talk, her robe slips open, and it's quite obvious that she has nothing on underneath. Jason breaks out in a sweat trying to maintain eye contact. After a few minutes, she places her hand on his arm and says, "Let's go into my apartment. I hear someone coming . . ."

Jason follows her into the apartment. Once inside, she leans against the wall, allowing her robe to fall off completely. Now completely nude, she purrs, "What would you say is my best feature?"

The flustered, embarrassed Jason clears his throat several times and finally blurts out, "Your ears!"

She's stunned! "My ears? Looks at these breasts! They're full and they're 100 percent natural! My butt is firm and doesn't sag, and I have great legs! Why in the world would you say my ears are my best feature?"

Clearing his throat once again, Jason stammers, "Because, when we were in the hallway, you said you heard someone coming. That was me!"

🎭

A woman tells her friend, "My husband bought me a mood ring the other day. When I'm in a really good mood, it turns green. When I'm in a really bad mood, it leaves a red mark on his forehead."

🎭

Lenny was delighted when he found a young woman who accepted his proposal of marriage. It seems he was sensitive about his wooden leg and a bit afraid that no one would have him at all. In fact, he couldn't bring himself to tell his fiancée about his leg when he slipped the ring on her finger, nor when she bought the dress, nor even when they picked the time and place for the wedding.

All he kept saying was, "Darling, I've got a big surprise for you," at which she blushed and smiled.

At long last, the wedding day came, and after the ceremony the young couple were alone in their hotel room.

"Now don't forget, Lenny, you promised me a big surprise," said the bride.

Still embarrassed and unable to tell her, Lenny turned out the lights, unstrapped his wooden leg, slipped into bed, and placed his wife's hand on the stump.

"Hmmmmmm," she said softly, "This *is* a surprise. Pass me the jar of Vaseline and I'll see what I can do!"

Q: WHY DO MEN WANT TO MARRY VIRGINS?
A: They can't stand criticism.

An old man was riding on a city bus. The bus stopped at a regular stop along its route. A young punk rocker got on and sat down across from the old man. The punk had spiked, rainbow-colored hair, along with dangling feathered earrings.

The young man, noticing that the old man was staring at him, finally became disgusted and said, "Old man, what the hell are you staring at? Didn't you ever do anything wild when you were young and full of life like me?"

The old man replied, "Yes, I once fucked a parrot. I was trying to decide if you might be my son."

A woman recently lost her husband. She had him cremated and brought his ashes home. Picking up the urn that he was in, she poured him out onto the counter. Then, while tracing her fingers in the ashes, she started talking to him. "Douglas, you know that fur coat you promised me? I bought it with the insurance money!

"Douglas, remember that new car you promised me? Well, I also bought it with the insurance money!

"Douglas, that emerald necklace you promised me? I bought it, too, with the insurance money."

Still tracing her finger in the ashes, she said, "Douglas, remember that blow job I promised you? Here it comes."

A woman accompanied her husband to the doctor's office. After his checkup, the doctor called the wife into his office alone. He said, "Your husband is suffering from a very severe nervous disorder. If you don't reduce his stress, your husband will surely die.

"Every morning," he continued, "fix him a big breakfast. Be accommodating at all times. For lunch, make him a nutritious meal. For dinner, prepare a three-course meal for him. Take on his chores. No nagging. And most importantly, make love with your husband every night—twice on weekends. If you can do this for the next year, I think your husband will regain his health completely."

On the way home, the husband asked his wife, "What did the doctor say when he asked to see you alone?"

"He said you're going to die," she replied.

Sign Number 17 she is getting bored with sex:

She bangs her head on the headboard before the guy gets in bed.

This jock is taken into a lineup for a rape case, and when they bring the victim in to pick out her attacker, he starts jumping up and down and shouting, "That's her! That's her!"

Four surgeons were sitting around discussing who they prefer to operate on.

The first surgeon said, "I like operating on librarians. When you open them up, everything is in perfect alphabetical order."

The second surgeon said, "I like operating on accountants. When you open them up, everything is in numerical order."

The third surgeon said, "I like operating on electricians. When you open them up, everything is color-coded."

The fourth surgeon said, "I like operating on lawyers."

The other three surgeons looked at each other in disbelief. One of them asked why.

The fourth surgeon replied, "Because they are heartless, gutless, spineless, and their asses and heads are interchangeable."

A man, feeling frisky, says to his wife, "Want a quickie?"

She replies, "You mean there's a choice?"

A woman goes into a bar with a little poodle on a leash. She sits down at the bar next to a drunk.

The drunk leans over, and *barf!* He pukes all over the dog. The drunk looks down, sees the little dog struggling in the pool of vomit, and slurs, "When the hell did I eat that?"

In a rare moment of tenderness, a husband whispers to his wife, "I love you terribly."

She replies, "Well, I'm glad you can finally admit it."

A man is in his front yard attempting to fly a kite with his son. Every time the kite gets up into the air, it comes crashing down. This goes on for a while, until his wife sticks her head out of the front door and yells, "You need more tail."

The father yells back, "Fuck you! I told you yesterday I needed more tail and you told me to go fly a kite!"

A newlywed couple just moved into their new house. One day the husband comes home from work and his wife says, "Honey, you know, in the upstairs bathroom one of the pipes is leaking, could you fix it?"

The husband just looks at his wife and says, "Who do I look like, Mr. Plumber?"

A few days go by, and he comes home from work and again his wife asks for a favor. "Honey, the car won't start, I think that it needs a new battery. Could you change it for me?"

"Who do I look like, Mr. Goodwrench?" is his response.

Another couple of weeks go by, and it's raining pretty

hard. His wife then finds a leak in the roof. She pleads with him as he's walking through the door. "Honey, there's a leak on the roof! Can you please fix it?"

He just looks at her and says, "Who do I look like, Bob Vila?" and sits down with a beer and watches a game on TV.

One weekend the husband wakes up and it's pouring pretty hard, but the leak on the roof is gone! Speaking of leaks, when he goes to take a shower, he finds that the one pipe behind the sink isn't leaking anymore either.

His wife was coming home just then, and as she walks through the door, the husband asks, "Honey, how come there aren't any more leaks, and the car's running?"

She replies nonchalantly, "Oh, the other day I was picking up the mail, and I ran into one of our new neighbors, Jon. What a nice man. He came over and fixed everything."

"Wow, did he charge us anything?" asks the husband.

"No, he just said that he'd do it for free if I either baked him a cake or had sex with him" she says.

"That's great. What kind of cake did you make?" asks the husband.

"Cake?" answers his wife. "Who the hell do you think I am—Betty Crocker?"

There were three rednecks in New York City. One day, while sightseeing, they came upon a whorehouse. Excited, they entered the whorehouse like kids going into a toy store for the very first time.

The first redneck had five dollars, the second redneck had ten dollars, and the third redneck had fifteen dollars.

The first redneck approached the lady behind the desk and said, "I got five dollars! What do I get for five dollars?"

The lady spoke over the intercom and said, "Ginger, take this gentleman upstairs and give him five dollars' worth!"

Sometime later, the first redneck came back downstairs, grinning from ear to ear.

One of the other two rednecks said, "What did you get for five dollars?"

The first redneck explained that the whore took it out of his pants, put whipped cream all over his privates, and then licked it all off.

This excited the second redneck and he quickly approached the lady at the desk. He said, "Okay, I have ten dollars! What do I get for ten dollars?"

The lady spoke over the intercom and said, "Tasha, take this gentleman upstairs and give him ten dollars' worth!"

When the second redneck came back downstairs, he had a huge grin on his face.

The first met him and asked, "Man, what did you get for ten dollars?"

The second redneck explained that the whore took it out of his pants, put whipped cream on it, along with nuts and chocolate topping, and then she licked it all off.

This excited the third redneck, so he nervously approached the lady at the desk and said, "I have fifteen dollars. What can I get for fifteen dollars?"

The lady turned on the intercom again and said, "Melissa, take this gentleman upstairs and give him fifteen dollars' worth!"

Afterward, the third redneck came downstairs with a huge frown on his face, and on the brink of tears.

Curious, the other two rednecks both asked, "Why are you so sad? What could've gone wrong? You had fifteen dollars."

The third redneck said, "Boys, she took it out of my pants and put whipped cream all over it. Then she put strawberries, pineapple topping, chocolate syrup, nuts, and a big cherry on top! But it looked so good, I ate it myself."

A study by federal transportation engineers involved installing microphones in all new vehicles made in the past four years. The devices revealed that the most common words uttered by a driver before a fatal accident were, "Oh, shit."

Except south of the Mason-Dixon Line, where the words were more likely to be, "Hey, fellas! Watch this!"

Q: HOW DO YOU CASTRATE A REDNECK?
A: Kick his sister in the jaw.

After closing time, an armed man is robbing a bar.

"Give me all your money," he yells.

"Anything," the bartender says, "just don't kill me."

"And throw all those antique coins in the bag, too."

"I will," the bartender says, "just don't shoot me."

"And give me a blow job," the robber demands.

"Anything you say," the bartender says, unzipping the robber's pants. The robber is so excited that he drops his gun halfway through it.

The bartender grabs the pistol and shoves it back in the guy's hand.

"Hold on to that," the bartender says. "One of my friends might walk in."

Q: WHAT DID ADAM SAY UPON SEEING EVE FOR THE FIRST TIME?
A: Stand back—I don't know how big this thing gets!

Q: WHAT DO MOST MEN USE FOR BIRTH CONTROL?
A: Their personalities.

Q: HOW ARE MEN LIKE PARKING SPACES?
A: The good ones are usually taken, and all the available ones are either handicapped or too small.

His first day in second grade, Johnny listened as the other children struggled to count to forty. When it was his turn, he counted all the way to sixty-five. His teacher said, "Well done," and after school he bragged about it to his father.

"That's because you're from Arkansas, son," the father told him.

The next day, the children had trouble reading a short story all the way through, but Johnny knew more words than any of them.

"That's because you're from Arkansas, son," his dad told him that afternoon.

The next day was gym class, and Johnny noticed his cock was much longer than any of the other boys'.

"Is that because I'm from Arkansas, Daddy?" Johnny asked at dinner that night.

"No, son," his father replied. "That's because you're sixteen."

Q: WHY DID THE MAN CROSS THE ROAD?
A: He heard the chicken was a slut.

One day the Arkansas county sheriff sees Bunky walking around town with nothing on except his boots.

The sheriff says, "Bunky, what the hell are you doing walking around town dressed like that?"

Bunky replies, "Well, Sheriff, me and Sarah Lou was down on the farm and we started a-cuddlin'. Sarah Lou said we should go inside the barn, and we did. Inside the barn we stated a-kissing and a-cuddlin' some more, and things got pretty hot and heavy. Well, then Sarah Lou took off all her clothes and said that I should do the same. So I took off all my clothes except my boots. Then Sarah Lou lay herself on the hay and said. 'Okay, Bunky, let's go to town!' and I guess I'm the first one to get here."

Three mice are at a bar, having drinks, talking about how tough they are. The first mouse slams down a shot of booze, says, "Let me tell you how tough I am. I spot a trap and go for the cheese. When it snaps, I snatch the bar and bench press it twenty or so times, and then before it can close I'm outta there!" And he tosses down another shot.

The second mouse slams down a shot and says, "You think that's tough? When I find a pile of rat poison, I crush it and snort it like it's cocaine." With that, he throws down another shot and slams his glass down on the bar.

The first two are staring at the third mouse, waiting to see what he has to say for himself. He throws down a shot of booze, puts his glass on the counter, and heads for the door. His buddies look at each other, then at him, and say, "What, no story from you?"

"I haven't got time for this shit," the third mouse says. "I need to get home to screw the cat."

※

A newly married sailor was informed by the navy that he was going to be stationed a long way from home on a remote island in the Pacific for a year. A few weeks after he got there, he began to miss his new wife, so he wrote her a letter. "My love," he wrote, "we are going to be apart for a very long time. Already I'm starting to miss you and there's really not much to do here in the evenings. Besides that, we're constantly surrounded by young attractive native girls. A hobby of some sort would certainly help me resist temptation."

So his wife sent him back a harmonica, saying, "Why don't you learn to play this?"

Eventually, his tour of duty came to an end and he rushed back to his wife. "Darling," he said, "I can't wait to get you into bed so that we make passionate love!"

She kissed him and said, "First let's see you play that harmonica."

※

A redneck girl was dating a fellow in Pennsylvania named Clarence. They got into a huge fight and she told her two brothers, Elmer and Bucky, about it. They jumped into their pickup truck and headed to Pennsylvania to settle the score with Clarence. They reached the state line, and after driving under an overpass, Bucky made a quick U-turn and headed back home quickly.

Surprised, Elmer said, "Why'd you turn around?"

Bucky replied, "I ain't messing around with that dude. Did you see that sign back there? It said, 'Clearance fourteen feet eight inches.' "

Q: WHY DID THE CONDOM CROSS THE ROAD?
A: It was pissed off.

There were four guys sitting in a bar. One of them asks what they think is the fastest thing in the world.

The first guy says, "I think a Concord jet is the fastest thing in the world, because it can go faster than the speed of sound."

The second guy says, "I think lightning is the fastest thing in the world, because it can go faster than the speed of sound *and* light."

The third guy says, "Nope. The brain is the fastest thing in the world, because whenever you need it to think of something, it is right there for you."

Then the fourth guys speaks up. "I think the anal sphincter is the fastest thing on earth."

"Really?" the others say. "Why?"

"I was actually on the Concord not too long ago," the fourth guy says. "It got struck by lightning and I couldn't think of what to do. But right away, I shit my pants."

Q: WHAT'S PINK AND HARD AND DRIPS WHEN IT GETS PUMPED UP?
A: A weight-lifting pig.

A salesman was given a hotel room next to one occupied by honeymooners. The walls were thin, and the sounds of lovemaking just passed through the walls as if they weren't even there. Finally, the salesman couldn't stand it any longer. He pounded on the wall, yelling, "Knock it off—there's other people trying to get some sleep!"

From the other room came a weak, faltering male voice, which said, "Yell louder, mister, she can't hear you!"

Boys will be boys, but someday girls will be women.

Two friends are talking about how they'd prefer to go when they have to die someday. One says to the other, "When I die, I want to go like my grandfather. Peaceful and asleep. Not screaming, like all the other people in his car."

Q: HOW DO MOST MEN STAY TRIM AND FIT?
A: By lying their asses off.

The doctor took Stan into the room and said, "Stan, I have some good news and some bad news."

Stan said, "Give me the good news."

"They're going to name a disease after you."

A cop stops his patrol car when he sees a couple sitting on the curb. The guy is lying on his side with his pants pulled down, the girl has her finger in his asshole, and she is thrusting with some enthusiasm.

The cop says, "What the hell is going on?"

The girl says, "This is my first date with this jerk. When I told him I wouldn't spend the night with him, he started pouring the booze down his throat. Now he's too drunk to drive me home, so I'm trying to sober him up. I'm gonna make him puke."

Skeptical, the cop says, "That's not going make him puke."

She says, "Oh yeah? Just wait till I switch this finger to his mouth!"

Two virgins get married. Their first morning together, the bride looks up and says, "You know, you really are a terrible lover."

The man frowns and replies, "How can you tell after just thirty seconds?"

An old man sat on a park bench crying. A younger man walked up to him and asked, "What's wrong?"

The old man replied, "I am married to a sexy twenty-one-year-old woman who gives me two blow jobs a day and we have sex the minute I get home from work and right after dinner."

The young man got a strange look on his face and asked, "What's so bad about that? It sounds to me like you have a great sex life."

The old man replied, "I can't remember where I live!"

A man and his wife are fucking.

Fifteen minutes have passed, thirty minutes, then forty-five minutes. Sweat is pouring off both of them.

The wife finally looks up and says, "What's the matter, darling, can't you think of anyone else, either?"

❖

A teacher notices that a little boy at the back of the class is squirming around, scratching his crotch, and not paying attention. She goes back to find out what's wrong. He's quite embarrassed and whispers that he has just recently been circumcised and his privates are itching.

The teacher has him go down to the principal's office to phone his mom and ask her what he should do about it. He does this and returns to the class and sits down in his seat, when suddenly there's a general commotion at the back of the room. Back down she goes, only to find him sitting at his desk with his penis hanging out.

"I thought I told you to call your mom," she says.

"I did," he says. "And she told me that if I could stick it out till noon, she'd come and pick me up from school."

❖

God calls down to Adam one day.

"I've got good news and bad news, Adam. The good news: I'm giving you both a penis and a brain. The bad news: They both can't run at the same time."

❖

A businessman returns from the Far East. After a few days, he notices a strange growth on his penis. He sees several doctors. They all say: "You've been screwing around in the Far East, very common there, no cure. We'll have to cut it off." The man panics, but figures if it is common in the East, they must know how to cure it there. So he goes back and sees a doctor in Thailand.

The doctor examines him and says, "You've been fooling around in my country. This is a very common problem here. Did you see any other doctors?"

The man replies, "Yes, a few in the USA."

The doctor says, "I bet they told you it had to be cut off."

The man answers, "Yes!"

The doctor smiles, nods. "That is not correct."

"Thank God," the man says. "I don't know what I would do without it, and my wife would leave me."

"It will fall off by itself," the doctor said.

A guy walks into a bar and sits down. He says to the bartender, "I'll have a rum and orange juice."

The bartender reaches behind the bar and pulls up an apple. The guy says, "What the hell is this?"

The bartender says, "Try it. Take a bite out of one side of the apple."

The man bites it, and finds it tastes like rum.

The bartender says, "Now try the other side of the apple."

The guy tries the other side, and damn, it tastes like an orange.

Impressed, the man says, "Okay, now I'd like a gin and tonic."

The bartender pulls up another apple. The man bites each side, one side tasting like gin, the other like tonic.

Now really impressed, the man says, "Have you got anything that tastes like pussy?"

"Sure," the bartender says, pulling out yet another apple.

The man eagerly bites into the apple, then spits it out. He says, "Damn, that tastes like shit!"

The bartender says, "Try the other side."

Q: WHY IS URINE YELLOW AND SPERM WHITE?
A: So men can tell when they're coming and going.

Two airplane mechanics named Dave and Bart work at the Atlanta airport. Atlanta gets fogged in one night and nothing can take off or land, so Dave and Bart have nothing to do. After work Dave and Bart usually have a drink on their way home, so Dave says to Bart, "I heard that you can get a buzz off drinking jet fuel." Since they have nothing better to do, they try it. Finally, their shift is over and they get to go home.

Next morning Dave calls Bart and says, "How are you feeling?" Bart says he's fine, never felt better. Dave asks, "Do you have a hangover?" Bart says no.

Then Bart says, "Wow this is great! We can drink all we want and not get a hangover."

Then Dave says, "Well, there is one side effect, Bart. Have you farted yet?"

Bart says, "No, why?"

Dave says, "I'm calling you from Detroit!"

A Men's Glossary:

"I'm hungry." = I'm hungry.

"I'm sleepy." = I'm sleepy.

"I'm tired." = I'm tired.

"Do you want to go to a movie?" = I'd like to have sex with you.

"Can I take you out to dinner?" = I'd like to have sex with you.

"Can I call you sometime?" = I'd like to have sex with you.

"May I have this dance?" = I'd like to have sex with you.

"Nice dress!" = Nice cleavage.

"You look tense, let me give you a massage." = I want to fondle you.

"What's wrong?" = What meaningless self-inflicted psychological trauma are you going through now?

"What's wrong?" = I guess sex tonight is out of the question.

"I'm bored." = Do you want to have sex?

"I love you." = Let's have sex now.

"I love you, too." = Can we move on to oral?

"Yes, I like the way you cut your hair." = I liked it better before.

"Yes, I like the way you cut your hair." = Fifty dollars and it doesn't look that much different!

"Let's talk." = I am trying to impress you by showing that I am a deep person and maybe then you'd like to have sex with me.

"Will you marry me?" = You win.

A recent survey found that 70 percent of married men cheat in America. The other 30 percent cheat in Europe.

A new guy in town walks into a bar and reads a sign that hangs over the bar: FREE BEER FOR THE PERSON WHO CAN PASS THE TEST! So the guy asks the bartender what the test is. The bartender says, "Well, first you have to drink that whole gallon of tequila. Then there's a crocodile out back with a sore tooth you have to remove. Then there's a woman upstairs who's never had an orgasm, and you have to give her one."

"I'll do it," the man says. He downs the entire gallon of tequila. Finished, he wipes his lips, staggers out of the bar, and yells, "Wherezdatallergatah?"

He tromps off into the swamp, and within ten minutes, the patrons hear a horrible roar. The man comes back with a torn shirt and no pants. "Now wherez . . . dat . . . woman . . . with . . . a . . . sore . . . tooth?"

A young single guy is on a cruise ship, having the time of his life. On the second day of the cruise, the ship slams into an iceberg and begins to sink. Passengers around him are screaming, flailing, and drowning, but the young guy manages to grab onto a piece of driftwood and, using all his strength, swims a few miles through the shark-infested sea to a remote island.

Sprawled on the shore, nearly dead from exhaustion, he turns his head and sees a woman lying near him, unconscious, barely breathing. She has also washed up on shore from the sinking ship. He makes his way toward her, and using mouth-to-mouth resuscitation, he manages to get her breathing again. She looks up at him, wide-eyed and grateful, and says, "My God, you saved my life!"

He suddenly realizes the woman is Cindy Crawford!

Days and weeks go by. Cindy and the young guy are living on the island together. They've set up a hut, there's fruit on the trees, and they're in heaven. Cindy's fallen madly in love with our man, and they're making passionate love morning, noon and night. Alas, one day she notices he's looking kind of glum.

"What's the matter, sweetheart?" she asks. "We have a wonderful life together. I'm in love with you. Is there something wrong? Is there anything I can do?"

He says, "Actually, Cindy, there is. Would you mind putting on my shirt?"

"I don't mind," she says, "if it will help." He takes off his shirt and she puts it on.

"Now would you put on my pants?" he asks.

"Sure, honey, if it's really going to make you feel better," she says.

"Okay, would you put on my hat now, and draw a little mustache on your face?" he asks.

"Whatever you want, sweetie," she says, and does.

Then he says, "Now, would you start walking around the edge of the island?"

She starts walking around the perimeter of the island. He sets off in the other direction. They meet up halfway around the island a few minutes later. He rushes up to her, grabs her by the shoulders, and says, "Dude! You'll never believe who I'm sleeping with!"

※

A man is talking to his therapist, who asks him if he talks to his wife during sex.

"Sometimes I do now," says the man. "Ever since I bought a cell phone."

⚜

An elephant is howling with pain in the jungle when a mouse comes along.

"I'll get that thorn out of your foot," the mouse says. "But you have to let me fuck you."

"Fine," says the elephant.

So the mouse climbs up the elephant's tail and mounts it. As he does, a coconut falls from the tree and nails the elephant in the head, causing it to flail its trunk and roar.

"Yeah, bitch," the mouse shouts. "Take it all."

⚜

"This day holds a lot of meaning for me," says a woman to her friend on a special day. "It was on this day two years ago that I lost my dear husband. I'll never forget that game of cards . . ."

⚜

There was a world-famous painter who, at the height of her career, started losing her eyesight. Fearful that her career as a painter might end, she went to see the best eye surgeon in the world. After delicate surgery and several weeks of therapy, her eyesight was restored. The painter was so grateful that she decided to show her gratitude by repainting the doctor's office. Part of her work included painting a gigantic eye on one wall. When she had finished her work, she held a press conference to unveil her latest work of art: the doctor's office.

During the press conference, one reporter noticed the eye on the wall and asked the doctor, "What was your first reaction upon seeing your newly painted office, especially that large eye on the wall?"

"Thank God I'm not a gynecologist."

🛡️

A doctor comes out to talk to a woman about her ailing husband. "He is either in the early stages of AIDS or Alzheimer's."

"You can't tell which?" the wife asks.

"Not really," he says. "Tell you what. Take him for a long drive in the country, then throw him out of the car. If he makes it back, don't fuck him."

🛡️

An elderly couple is watching a television preacher one night who says, "Friends, I have the power to heal the sick. I want you to put one hand on the television and one hand on the part of the body that ails you while I pray."

The husband stands up, puts a hand on the television and his other on his groin.

His wife says, "He's talking about healing the sick, dear, not raising the dead."

🛡️

A man has three girlfriends but can't decide which to marry. So he gives them each five thousand dollars and decides to see how they will spend it. The first gets a full makeover.

"I wanted myself to look beautiful for you," she says.

The second buys him new clothes and golf clubs.

"I bought you these gifts because I love you so much," she says.

The third puts it all in a mutual fund, saying, "I wanted to invest for our future together."

The man thinks about all three women and the decision each made, and then he marries the one with the biggest tits.

An elderly couple was driving cross-country, and the man was at the wheel.

He gets pulled over by a female trooper. The officer says, "Sir, did you know you were speeding?"

The man turns to his wife and asks, "What did she say?"

The old woman yells, "SHE SAYS YOU WERE SPEEDING."

The officer says, "May I see your license?"

The man turns to his wife and asks, "What did she say?"

The old woman yells, "SHE WANTS TO SEE YOUR LICENSE."

The man gives her his license.

The trooper says, "I see you are from Maryland. I spent some time there once, had the worst sex with a man I have ever had."

The man turns to his wife and asks, "What did she say?"

"SHE THINKS SHE KNOWS YOU," the old woman yells.

Sarah goes up to Father O'Grady after his Sunday-morning service, and she's in tears.

He says, "So what's bothering you, dear?"

She says, "Oh, Father, I've got terrible news. My husband passed away last night."

The priest says, "Oh, Sarah, that's awful. Tell me, Sarah, did he have any last requests?"

She says, "That he did, Father."

The priest says, "What did he ask, Sarah?"

"He said, 'Please, Sarah, put down the goddamn gun . . .' "

A chicken and an egg lay in bed together. The chicken was smiling and smoking a cigarette, but the egg looked very distraught. "Well," said the egg, frowning, "I guess that answers that question!"

A man is so ashamed at his small penis that he can't bring himself to have sex. But he finally meets a nurse who is too irresistible, and he winds up in bed with her.

He warns her about his size, but she removes his shorts and says, "Oh, I've seen much smaller than that."

"Really?" the relieved man says.

"Of course," she replies. "I used to work in a maternity ward."

The room was full of pregnant women and their husbands in a Lamaze class. The instructor was reviewing health and lifestyle tips with the class.

"Ladies, exercise is good for you," announced the teacher. "Walking is great exercise. And fathers, it wouldn't hurt you to walk along with your wives."

A man in the middle of the group raised his hand.

"Yes?" asked the instructor.

"Is it all right if she carries a golf bag while we walk?"

A henpecked husband was advised by a psychiatrist to a himself more. "You don't have to let your wife bully you, said. "Now go home and show her you're the boss."

The husband decided to take the doctor's advice.

He went home, slammed the door, shook his fist in his wife's face, and growled, "From now on you're taking orders from me! I want my supper right now, and when you get it on the table, go upstairs and lay out my clothes. Tonight I am going out with the boys. You are going to stay at home, where you belong. And another thing—do you know who is going to zip my zipper for me?"

"I most certainly do," said his wife. "The undertaker."

Q: WHY DO POLLS SHOW MEN WOULDN'T MIND A FEMALE PRESIDENT?
A: Because you could pay her half as much.

A man lies on his deathbed, surrounded by his family—his weeping wife and four children. Three of the children are tall, good-looking, and athletic, but the fourth is an ugly runt.

"Darling," the husband whispers, "promise me that the youngest child really is mine. I want to know the truth before I die. I will forgive you if only you tell me the truth."

The wife gently says, "My dearest, I swear on my mother's grave that you are his father."

The man then dies, happy. The wife mutters under her breath, "Thank God he didn't ask about the other three."

Q: WHAT'S A WOMAN'S DEFINITION OF A MAN?

A: A support system for a penis.

Mr. Murdoch got himself a new secretary. She was young, sweet, and very polite. One day while taking dictation, she noticed his fly was open. When leaving the room, she said, "Mr. Murdoch, your barracks door is open."

He did not understand her remark, but later on he happened to look down and saw that his zipper was open.

He decided to have some fun with his secretary. Calling her in, he asked, "By the way, Miss Sarah, when you saw my barracks door was open this morning, did you also notice a soldier standing at attention?"

The secretary replied, "Why no, sir, all I saw was a little disabled veteran sitting on two duffel bags, with his head down."

Q: WHAT'S THE DEFINITION OF A MAN WITH CLASS?

A: He gets out of the shower to pee.

Fred was unable to satisfy his blond wife. He tried all the positions but just couldn't do it. He finally went to his best friend and asked for advice.

The friend said, "Hire a well-hung young stud to stand near your bed and wave a big towel over both of you while you are having sex, like a Roman slave. Your wife is bound to be turned on to the point that she can come."

The guy hired the stud, but all efforts were in vain. He

went back to his friend and told him what happened. So his friend suggested that they switch places.

"Why don't you wave the towel while the stud does the job in bed?" said the friend. Fred agreed, saying that he would do anything to satisfy his wife. He hired the same guy again, and this time they traded positions. Naturally, the blonde had a divine orgasm.

As she screamed, the husband leaned over to the stud and said, "You see! That's how you wave the fucking towel!"

Q: WHAT'S THE DIFFERENCE BETWEEN A PENIS AND A PAY-CHECK?

A: It's easy to blow a paycheck.

A woman goes into a tattoo parlor and tells the artist that she wants a tattoo of a turkey on her right thigh just below her bikini line. She also wants him to put *Happy Thanksgiving* under the turkey.

So the guy does it and it comes out looking really good. The woman then instructs him to put a Santa tattoo with *Merry Christmas* up on her left thigh. So the guy does it and it comes out looking perfect, too.

As the woman is getting dressed to leave, the tattoo artist asks, "If you don't mind, could you tell me what those tattoos are for?"

She says, "I'm sick and tired of my husband complaining all the time that there's nothing good to eat between Thanksgiving and Christmas."

---

young guy was lying on his back on a massage table, wearing only a towel over his groin. A young, very attractive Japanese girl was massaging his shoulders, then his chest, and gradually working her way down his torso. The guy was getting sexually excited as the masseuse approached the towel. The towel began to lift and the Japanese girl arched her eyebrows.

"You want a hand job?" she asked.

"You bet," came the excited reply.

"Okay," she said. "I come back in ten minutes."

Two guys are leaving work when one says: "The first thing I'm going to do when I get home is rip my wife's panties off."

"You're that horny?"

"No, the elastic is killing me."

A man and his friends walk into a bar and sit down. They all order drinks and are having a good time when an incredibly drunk man walks in. The drunk points a finger at the man and says, "Your mom's a whore." Everyone in the bar gets quiet, expecting a fight. But the man just sits there looking at his drink, so the drunk walks away and things return to normal.

Ten minutes later the drunk comes back, points to the same guy, and says, "Your mom is the best lay in town." Again everyone pauses, expecting a fight. But the man just sits there looking down at his drink, so the drunk walks away again.

But ten minutes later he walks back over, points to the guy, and says, "I banged your mom tonight, and damn, was she nasty!"

That was it. The guy throws down his drink, stands up,

grabs the drunk by the collar, and yells, "Dad, you're drunk! Go home!"

Stan complained to his friend Irving that lovemaking to his wife was becoming routine and boring.

"Get creative, Stan. Break up the monotony. Why don't you try 'playing doctor' for an hour? That's what I do," said Irving.

"Sounds great," Stan replied, "but how do you make it last for an hour?"

"Just keep her in the waiting room for fifty-five minutes!" said Irving.

Three guys go to a ski lodge where there aren't enough rooms, so they have to share a bed. In the middle of the night, the guy on the right wakes up and says, "I had this wild, vivid dream of getting a hand job!"

The guy on the left wakes up, and unbelievably, he's had the same dream.

Then the guy in the middle wakes up and says, "That's funny, I dreamed I was skiing!"

An investment banker catches his wife in bed with another man.

He says to her, "What are you doing?"

She says, "I've gone public!"

A man comes home from work and finds his wife giving the paperboy a blow job.

"Honey," he demanded, "what are you doing? You know it's the plumber we owe!"

⚜

Two guys are wiling away their lunch hour in a rural bar. One looks out the window at a herd of sheep.

"Man, I sure wish those sheep were women," he says.

"I just wish it was dark," says the other.

⚜

A young man is talking to his father, a retired air-force colonel, about his first days as an airborne recruit.

"Dad, it was awful. We were up in the plane for our first jump, and our sergeant was giving us this frightening speech. He grabbed a big nightstick and said, 'The first son of a bitch who decides he can't jump out of this plane is going to get this shoved hard up his ass.' We all stared at one another, and then the doors opened and I was the first one to have to go."

"You jumped?" his father asked.

"Just a little."

⚜

A married man was visiting his girlfriend one day when she requested that he shave his beard. "Oh, Kirk, I like your beard, but I would really love to see your handsome face."

Kirk replied, "I couldn't possibly do it. My wife loves this beard—she would kill me!"

"Oh, please?" the girlfriend asked again, in a sexy little voice.

"But my wife loves it!" he said.

The girlfriend asked once more, and he sighed and fi̅
gave in.

That night, Kirk crawled into bed with his wife while she
was sleeping.

The wife stirred, felt his clean-shaven face, and said, "Oh,
Michael, you shouldn't be here. My husband will be home
soon!"

Q: How many Real Women does it take to screw in a lightbulb?

A: None. A Real Woman would have a man around to do it.

A man was driving down a quiet country lane when out into
the road strayed a rooster. *Whack!* The rooster disappeared
under the car in a cloud of feathers. Shaken, the man pulled
over at the farmhouse and rang the doorbell. A farmer appeared. The man said, a bit nervously, "I think I killed your
rooster; please allow me to replace him."

"Suit yourself," the farmer replied. "The hens are 'round
the back."

A man walks into a bar and orders two drinks. As the bartender watches, he drinks one and pours the other on his hand.
Then he orders two more drinks and does the same thing.

The third time he does it, the bartender asks, "What are
you doing?"

The man smiles at him, winks, and says, "I'm trying to get
my date drunk."

Two women are catching up at their twentieth high-school reunion. The conversation turns to sex.

"Things are fine, I guess," Carol says. "We usually do it on Sunday nights and alternating Wednesdays."

"Wow," says Ellen. "We're just into S&M."

"S&M? Wow!" says Carol.

"Yeah," Ellen says, "he Snores and I Masturbate."

A doctor tells a woman she can no longer touch anything alcoholic. So she gets a divorce.

A man enters the hospital for a circumcision. When he comes to after the procedure, he's perturbed to see several doctors standing around his bed.

"Son, there's been a bit of a mix-up," admits the surgeon. "I'm afraid there was an accident, and we were forced to perform a sex-change operation. You now have a vagina instead of a penis."

"What!" gasps the patient. "You mean I'll never experience another erection?"

"Oh, you might," the surgeon reassures him. "Just not yours."

Q: WHAT DO YOU CALL A WOMAN WITHOUT AN ASSHOLE?
A: Divorced.

One day this cop pulls over a drunk for speeding. The cop gets out of his car and asks the guy for his license.

"You cops should decide what you want," the guy says. "One day you take away my license, and the next day you ask me to show it to you."

There are three guys talking in a bar. Two of them are talking about the amount of control they have over their wives, while the third remains silent.

After a while one of the two turns to the third and says, "Well, what about you? Are you the boss at home?"

"I'll tell you," the third fellow says. "Just the other night my wife came to me on her hands and knees."

The first two guys are amazed. "What happened then?" the second asks.

"She said, 'Get out from under the bed and fight like a man.'"

A father walks into the bathroom and catches his son masturbating. He starts yelling, "Son! How many times have I told you not to do that? Stop it! If you keep doing that, you'll go blind!"

The son replies, "I'm over here, Dad."

A wife is surprised to find her husband suddenly so interested in Mideast politics. He reads almost every article about it he can find. Finally, she asks him: "You do realize the Gaza Strip isn't a topless bar, don't you?"

🛡️

A small boy was lost, so he went up to a policeman.

"I've lost my dad!" he said.

The cop said, "What's he like?"

The little boy replied, "Beer and women."

🛡️

Q: WHY DID THE DRUNK TAKE A RIGHT INTO THE DITCH?
A: His blinker was on.

🛡️

A guy was sitting in the stadium at the Super Bowl in the very best seat available.

The man on his left noticed there was an empty seat next to him and said, "Can you believe someone actually paid for that seat and didn't come to the game?"

The guy replied, "Actually, that was for my wife. We bought these tickets months ago. Unfortunately, in the interim, my wife died, so I came alone."

"I'm sorry to hear that," said the man beside him. "But why didn't you give the ticket to a family member or a friend?"

"Oh, they're all at the funeral," said the guy.

🛡️

There was a middle-aged couple who had two stunningly beautiful blond teenage daughters. But they had always wanted a son, so they decided to try one last time for a boy.

After months of trying, the wife became pregnant, and sure enough, nine months later delivered a healthy baby boy. The joyful father rushed to the hospital nursery to see his new son. He took one look and was horrified to find the ugliest child he had ever seen. He went to his wife and said that there was no way he could be the father of that child.

"Look at the two beautiful daughters I fathered," he said, then stuck his face in his wife's, snarled, and added, "Have you been fooling around on me?"

She smiled and said, "Not this time, honey."

❦

Q: WHAT DO YOU GET WHEN YOU CROSS A MAN WITH A POTATO?
A: A dictator.

❦

An old man walks into a pharmacy and asks the guy behind the counter for some Viagra.

"How many would you like?" the pharmacist asks.

The old man replies, "Oh, I don't know, about three or so."

The man behind the counter laughs and says, "I don't think that'll do you much good."

The old man grunts and replies, "Listen, son, I'm eighty-four years old. I just want to be able to take a leak without pissing all over my shoes!"

❦

On doctor's orders, Merrick had moved to Florida. Two weeks later, he was dead. His body was shipped back home, where the undertaker prepared it for the funeral services.

Merrick's brother came in to make sure everything was

taken care of. "Would you like to see the body?" the undertaker asked.

"I might as well take a look at it before the others get here." The undertaker led him into the next room and opened the top half of the casket. He stood back and proudly displayed his work.

"He looks good," the brother said. "Those two weeks in Florida were just the thing for him."

Q: WHAT DO MOST MEN IN SINGLES BARS HAVE IN COMMON?
A: Wives.

As an elderly man drove down the freeway, his car phone rang.

Answering, he heard his wife's voice urgently warning him, "Franklin, I just heard on the news that there's a car going the wrong way on Route 280. Please be careful!"

"It's not just one car," said Franklin. "It's hundreds of them!"

Q: WHAT'S THE DIFFERENCE BETWEEN CELLULAR PHONES AND TAMPONS?
A: Cellular phones are for assholes.

A dedicated union worker was attending a convention in Las Vegas and, as you would expect, decided to check out the brothels nearby. When he got to the first one, he asked the madam, "Is this a union house?"

"No," she replied, "I'm sorry, it isn't."

"Well, if I pay you a hundred dollars, what cut does the girl get?"

"The house gets ninety and the girl gets ten."

Offended at such an unfair practice, the union man stomped off down the street in search of a more equitable, unionized shop. His search continued until finally he reached a brothel where the madam responded, "Why yes, sir, this *is* a union house."

The man asked, "And if I pay you a hundred dollars, what cut does the girl get?"

"The girl gets eighty, and the house gets twenty."

"That's more like it!" the union man said. He looked around the room and pointed to a stunningly attractive blonde. "I'd like her for the night."

"I'm sure you would, sir," said the madam, then, gesturing to a large fifty-five-year-old woman in the corner, "but Ethel here has seniority."

Mr. Potato Head is the perfect man: He's tan. He's cute. And if he looks at another girl, you can rearrange his face.

A woman enrolled in nursing school was attending an anatomy class. The subject of the day was involuntary muscles.

The instructor, hoping to liven up the class a bit, asked, "Do you know what your asshole does when you're having an orgasm?"

"Sure," the woman said. "He's at home, taking care of the kids."

A young couple was just married and spent their first wedding night with the young man's parents. In the morning, his mother got up and fixed breakfast. She went to the bottom of the stairs and called everyone to come down to eat. Everyone came down, except the newlyweds. After a long wait, the family ate without them.

The mother said, "I wonder why they never came down to eat."

The groom's young brother said, "Mommy, I think—"

"Oh, I don't want to hear any of your dirty thoughts," said the mother.

At lunchtime, the mother again prepared a wonderful spread and again called the young couple to eat. Five minutes went by and she called again. After another long wait, the family proceeded to eat.

As she was cleaning the table, the mother once again said, "I wonder why they never came down to eat."

Once again, the younger brother started to speak, but the mother immediately shut him up.

At dinner, the same thing happened. After the meal, the mother once again questioned why they had not come down to eat all day. The young lad once again said, "Mommy, I think—"

"Fine, what is it that you think?" asked the mother rather testily.

"I think that when he came down to get the Vaseline last night, he got my model airplane glue instead!"

A 500-pound man arrives at a weight-loss clinic and is ushered into a private room where a gorgeous brunette is waiting for him. "If you can catch me," she says, "you can make love to me."

After a chase that lasts ten minutes, he finally grabs her, and they have sex. He finds he has actually lost fifteen pounds in the process.

The next week, he comes back to the clinic and asks if it's possible to lose twenty-five pounds. Sure, the receptionist says, and she leads him to another room, where there is an even prettier blonde. "If you can catch me," she says, "you can make love to me."

After a thirty-minute chase, but even better sex, the man finds he has lost twenty-five pounds.

He comes back a third time and says he would like to lose a hundred pounds. The receptionist looks at him, then nods her head and leads him to a third room.

He opens it and finds an 800-pound woman who says, "I'm trying to lose weight, too!"

※

After spending a night at a hotel with a prostitute, the politician took $200 out of his wallet and placed it on the dressing table.

"Thanks," she said. "But I only charge twenty."

"Twenty bucks for the entire night?" the amazed politician asked. "You can't make a living on that."

"Oh, don't worry about me," the prostitute replied. "I do a little blackmail on the side!"

※

The five questions most feared by men are:

1. What are you thinking about?

2. Do you love me?

3. Do I look fat in this?

4. Do you think she is prettier than me?

5. Is it in yet?

🙶🙷

One evening, Brian O'Flannagan walked into a bar and ordered martini after martini, each time removing the olives and placing them in a jar. When the jar was filled with olives and all the drinks consumed, O'Flannagan started to leave.

"Excuse me," another customer said. "What is that all about?"

"Nothing," said the O'Flannagan. "My wife just sent me out for a jar of olives, so I'm taking these home."

🙶🙷

Two doctors—a man and a woman—at a medical conference start eyeing each other and wind up in the man's hotel room that night. After making love, they realize they know almost nothing about each other.

"I'll bet you're a surgeon," the man says to the woman.

She asks how he knew, and he says because she washed her hands twice when they got to the room.

"Good guess," she says. "And you're an anesthesiologist?"

"How did you know that?" he says, astonished.

"Because I didn't feel a thing."

🙶🙷

A man asks his father about sex in the twilight years.

"Well, when you're young, of course, it's every night in every position. Then it fades back to mostly missionary stuff once a week. For us, now, it's almost entirely oral."

"Oral?" the man says. "I had no idea."

"Yep," the father says. "I'm in my bedroom, she's in hers. And we both yell 'Fuck you!' at each other all the time."

Q: WHAT DO YOU CALL A REDNECK WITH A SHEEP UNDER EACH ARM?

A: A pimp.

A man travels to Spain and goes to a Madrid restaurant for a late dinner. He orders the house special and he is brought a plate with potatoes, corn, and two large meaty objects.

"What's this?" he asks.

"Cojones, señor," the waiter replies.

"What are cojones?" the man asks.

"Cojones," the waiter explains, "are the testicles of the bull who lost at the arena this afternoon."

At first the man is repulsed, but being the adventurous type, he decides to try this local delicacy. To his amazement, it is quite delicious.

In fact, the dish tastes so good that he decides to come back again the next night and order cojones again. After dinner the man informs the waiter that these were better than the pair he had the previous afternoon, but the portion was much smaller.

"Señor," the waiter says, "the bull does not lose every time."

When hunting season started, two men went out with their guns. When they got to a fork in the road near where they wanted to hunt, they saw a sign by the road that said BEAR LEFT. So they went home.

A little boy came home from school and asked his mother, "Mommy, is it true that babies come out of the same hole that the penis goes in?"

The mother, very surprised and more than a little embarrassed, replied, "Yes, dear, that's true."

The little boy, somewhat confused, asked, "Well, doesn't it knock your teeth out?"

Four men got together at a reunion. Three of them had sons and they started bragging about them, while the fourth guy went to the can to take a shit. The first man said his son was doing so well, he now owned a factory, manufacturing furniture. Why, just the other day he gave his best friend a whole house full of brand-new furniture.

The second man said his son was doing just as well. He was a manager at a car dealership. Why, just the other day he gave his best friend a Porsche. The third man said his son was doing well, too. He was a manager at a bank. Why, just the other day he gave his best friend the money to buy a house.

The fourth man came back, and the other three told him they were talking about how successful their sons are. He just shook his head and said his son was gay and hadn't amounted to much. But he must be doing something right, because just the other day, he was given a house, furniture, and a Porsche by his friends!

🃏

Son: Mommy, how do lions fuck?
Mother: I don't know. I've only fucked a pig.

🃏

Q: WHY DO MEN LIKE BLONDE JOKES?
A: They can understand them.

🃏

A lady walks into the dentist's office, takes off her underwear, sits down on the chair, and spreads her legs wide open.

"You must have made a mistake," says the shocked dentist. "The gynecologist's office is one floor above this one."

To that, the lady replies, "No mistake. You installed my husband's dentures last week; now you'll be the one getting them out."

🃏

A connoisseur walks into a bar and asks for a bottle of forty-year-old Scotch. The bartender, not wanting to give up the good liquor, pours a shot of ten-year-old Scotch and figures that the guy won't be able to tell the difference. The guy downs the Scotch and says: "This Scotch is only ten years old! I specifically asked for forty-year-old Scotch."

Amazed, the bartender reaches into a locked cabinet underneath the bar and pulls out a bottle of twenty-year-old Scotch and pours the man a shot. The guy drinks it down and says, "That was twenty-year-old Scotch. I asked for forty-year-old Scotch."

So the bartender goes into the back room and brings out a bottle of thirty-year-old Scotch and pours the guy a drink. By now a small crowd has gathered around the man and is watching anxiously as he downs the latest drink. Once again the guy states the true age of the Scotch and repeats his original request for forty-year-old Scotch.

The bartender can hold off no longer and disappears into the cellar to get a bottle of prime forty-year-old Scotch. Soon he returns with the bottle and pours a shot. The guy downs the Scotch and says, "Now THIS is forty-year-old Scotch!" The crowd applauds his expertise and his discriminating palate.

A drunk who has been watching the proceedings raises a full shot glass of his own and says, "Here, take a swig of this."

The connoisseur takes the glass and downs the drink in one swallow. Immediately he chokes and spits it out on the barroom floor. "My God! That tastes like piss," he coughs out.

"Sure," says the drunk. "But how old am I?"

Q: HOW ARE MEN AND WOMEN SIMILAR?
A: At thirty-five, women want to *have* children. At thirty-five, men want to *date* them.

Billy gets a call at home. A woman is crying on the other end.

"This is Sally."

"Sally?"

"Yes, you met me at Kevin's party two months ago. We were in the backseat your car, and you told me I was a good sport. Remember?"

"Not really."

"Well, I'm pregnant now, and I'm thinking about killing myself!"

"Say," Billy says, "you *are* a good sport."

⁂

A husband and wife got in a furious fight one night and agreed, for the sake of their marriage, not to speak to each other for a week. A few days into it, the man had an early sales call. His wife usually woke him for these, so he wrote her a note: "Please wake me at 7:00 A.M. tomorrow."

The next day, he awoke to a bright sun at 9:00 A.M. and found a note taped to his pillow: "Wake up. It's seven."

⁂

A young man is disappointed to see that his golfing partner for the day is a ninety-year-old man. Surprisingly, though, the old geezer seems to know what he's doing, making most pars and even offering some tips along the way. Toward the end of the nine holes, the young man finds himself on a tough par four.

"You know, when I was your age," the old man says, "I used to shoot the ball this way on this hole."

The young man takes his advice and drives the ball . . . right into a tree some fifty yards away.

"Of course," the old man says, "when I was your age, that tree was about waist-high."

⁂

"And will there be anything else, sir?" the bellboy asked after setting out an elaborate dinner for two in the lavish hotel room.

"No, thank you," the gentleman replied. "That will be all."

As the young man turned to leave, he noticed a beautiful satin negligee on the bed.

"Nothing for your wife?" he asked.

"Yeah! That's a good idea," the fellow said. "Please bring up a postcard."

Most men are like cement. After they're laid, it takes far too long for them to get hard.

Q: HOW MANY MEN DOES IT TAKE TO SCREW IN A LIGHT-BULB?

A: Three. One to screw it, another to try and sneak in the bedroom window and screw it himself, and a third to screw it once the other two are sick of it.

Q: DID YOU HEAR ABOUT THE MAN WHO SWALLOWED HIS VIAGRA TOO SLOWLY?

A: He got a stiff neck.

A jock walks into his history final with a pencil and a quarter. It's a true/false test, and he flips a coin for each answer. The professor watches this, and the guy finishes the last question before thirty minutes has even passed.

Then he turns back to the first question and starts flipping the coin again.

The professor says to him, "What are you doing?"

"Just checking my answers," the jock replies.

A big guy marries a tiny girl, and at the wedding, one of his friends says to him, "How the hell do the two of you have sex?"

The big guy says, "I just sit there, naked, on a chair, she sits on top, and I move her up and down."

His friend says, "That sounds a little tiring."

The big guy says, "Well, it's kind of like jerking off, only I've got somebody to talk to."

Two alien explorers are being debriefed on their home planet.

"Is there intelligent life on Earth?" the supervisor asks.

"Yes, there is," they reply. "And there's also a lot creatures with testicles."

Boys will be boys. But men are much better at it.

This guy went into a bar and ordered a beer. He happened to look down the bar and see a man sitting there with a head the size of a cue ball. So he walked down and said to the man, "Excuse me, sir, I don't mean to be rude, but I noticed you have a small head. Is that a birth defect?"

The man said, "No, I got it in the war. My ship was torpedoed and I was the only survivor on the ship, so I swam to shore. One day a mermaid swam up to me and said she would grant me three wishes. For my first wish I wanted to return home. The mermaid granted that wish. My second wish was to have all the money I would ever need. Wish granted. My third wish was to have sex with the mermaid. She said, 'I can't grant that wish because mermaids are fish below the waist, and so we can't have sex with humans.'

So I said, "How about a little head?"

Q: WHAT'S THE BEST THING TO DO IF YOUR HUSBAND WALKS OUT ON YOU?

A: Lock the door.

There's a guy in a bar, just looking at his drink.

He watches it for more than thirty minutes.

Then a big truck driver steps up next to him, takes the drink from the guy, and just knocks it back. The poor man starts crying.

The truck driver says, "Come on now, I was just joking. Here, I'll buy you another drink. I can't stand to see a grown man cry."

"No, it's not that. This day is the worst of my life. First, I fall asleep, and I get to my office late. My boss fires me. When I leave the building to get into my car, I find out it was stolen. The police say they can do nothing. I get a cab to return home, and when I leave it, I remember I left my wallet and credit cards in the cab. The cabdriver just drives away. I go inside my house, and when I get there, I find my wife in bed with the gardener. I leave home and come to this bar. When I finally get the nerve to kill myself, you come up and drink my poison."

A top banking executive had to spend a couple of [...] hospital. He was a royal pain to the nurses because [...] them around just like he did his employees. None [...] pital staff wanted to have anything to do with him. [...] nurse was the only one who could stand up to him.

She came into his room and announced, "I have to take your temperature."

After complaining for several minutes, he finally settled down, crossed his arms, and opened his mouth.

"No, I'm sorry," the nurse stated, "but for this reading, I cannot use an oral thermometer." This started another round of complaining, but eventually he rolled over and bared his rear end.

After the nurse inserted the thermometer, she announced, "I have to get something. Now you stay JUST LIKE THAT until I get back!"

She leaves the door to his room open on her way out. He curses under his breath as he hears people walking past his door laughing. After almost an hour, the man's doctor comes into the room. "What's going on here?" asks the doctor.

Angrily, the man answers, "What's the matter, Doc! Haven't you ever seen someone having their temperature taken?"

After a pause, the doctor confesses, "Well, no. I guess I haven't. Not with a carnation anyway."

A man sits down by a woman at a bar and says, "You know, this watch I'm wearing is magic. I can tell everything about someone by just looking at it."

"Prove it," she says.

"Well, for instance, I can tell that you're not wearing any panties."

"That's not true," she replies. "I am."

"Oops," he says, tapping the face of the watch. "This thing must be an hour fast."

❦

Q: YOUR HUSBAND IS AT THE FRONT DOOR WITH A CASE OF BEER IN HIS HANDS. YOUR DOG IS AT THE BACK DOOR, BEGGING TO COME IN. WHICH DOOR DO YOU OPEN FIRST?
A: The back door. At least the dog will stop whining once he's inside.

❦

Men come in three sizes: small, medium, and GOD YES!!!

❦

A guy sits down in a restaurant booth and accidentally knocks the spoon off the table. A waiter walking by immediately stops and pulls a spoon out of his pocket and sets it down. Impressed, the man asks if all waiters carry silverware with them.

"Yes," the waiter replies. "We hired an efficiency expert who calculated that 24.6 percent of all customers knock their spoons off the table when they first sit down. Carrying one with us saves five minutes and thirty-six seconds of our time each month."

Smiling, the man proceeds to eat the grilled-cheese-and-tomato-soup special and is ready to leave when he spots that same waiter walking from the register. There is a tiny white string dangling from his zipper that the man had not noticed before.

"Excuse me, waiter," he says. "But do you know you have a string hanging from your pants?"

"Yes," the waiter answers. "That same efficiency expert

found we waste seven minutes and twenty-six seconds a week washing our hands after using the restroom. So all the waiters tie strings to our dicks, and simply pull them out when it's time to go."

"Amazing," the man answers. Then he pauses. "Wait a minute. So how do you get your dick back in your pants?"

"I use a spoon," the waiter replies.

Arguing with his wife over bills, the husband finally exploded: "If it weren't for my money, the house wouldn't be here!"

The wife replied, "That's true. But if it weren't for your money, I wouldn't be here, either."

Q: WHY ARE MEN LIKE DIAPERS?
A: They're full of shit and always on your ass.

Q: WHAT'S THE CAUSE OF DEATH OF MEN'S BRAIN CELLS?
A: Boredom.

As a couple were driving home after a Christmas party, the woman asks her husband, "Honey, has anyone ever told you how handsome, sexy, and irresistible to women you are?"

A little bit tipsy, the flattered husband says, "No, dear, they haven't."

The wife yells, "Then what the hell gave you that idea at the party tonight?"

A man gets up early one morning and sees a Porsche advertised in the paper for $500. He can't believe it, but he drives to the address and finds a shiny, seemingly new Porsche in the driveway. A woman greets him and hands over the keys for a test drive. It runs perfectly.

"Why are you selling this for so little?" the man asks.

The woman smiles and says, "My husband just ran away with his secretary. He told me to keep the house and just sell the Porsche and send him the money."

Q: HOW MANY MARRIED MEN DOES IT TAKE TO SCREW IN A LIGHT BULB?

A: Wait a minute, didn't you say they were married?

These two guys had just gotten divorced and they swore they would never have anything to do with women again. They were best friends and they decided to move up to the Yukon as far north as they could go and never look at a woman again. They got up there and went into a trader's store and told him, "Give us enough supplies to last two men for one year." The trader got the gear together, and on top of each one's supplies he laid a board with a hole in it with fur around the hole.

The guys asked, "What's that board for?"

The trader said, "Well, where you're going there are no women and you might need this."

They said, "No way! We've sworn off women for life!"

The trader said, "Well, take the boards with you, and if you don't use them, I'll refund your money next year."

"Okay," they said, and left. The next year one of the guys

came into the trader's store and said, "Give me enough supplies to last one man for one year."

The trader said, "Weren't you in here last year with a partner?"

"Yeah," said the guy.

"Where is he?" asked the trader.

"I killed him," said the guy.

Shocked, the trader asks, "Why?"

To which the guy replies, "I caught him in bed with my board!"

Q: HOW DO YOU REALLY HURT A MAN WITH WORDS?
A: Slam a dictionary on his cock.

The postman is delivering a blowup party doll to an old man when he decides to test it out once in the truck. Then he returns it to the box and leaves it on the doorstep. A few months later, he sees the old man in the post office, returning the box to the manufacturer.

"Didn't like the doll, huh?" the guy asked.

"It was just too realistic," the old man said. "I actually got crabs from it."

Q: WHAT DO MEN AND MASCARA HAVE IN COMMON?
A: They both run at the first sign of any emotion.

Two girls are walking down the street early one morning when they notice a drunk wearing a kilt, passed out leaning against a lamppost. The first girl says to the second, "I hear they don't wear any underwear under those things. Go check!" So the second girl does, and sure enough, the guy isn't wearing any underwear.

The first girl takes a blue ribbon out of her hair and says, giggling, "Go tie this on his dick." The second girl does, and they walk off laughing.

Soon the drunk comes to and looks down at his dick with the ribbon on it. "Neat!" he says. "I don't know where I was last night, or what I did, but I'm glad I won first place!"

❧

A man and his wife are making love in the park when a bee suddenly flies into the woman's private parts. They rush her to an emergency room and explain the situation to the doctor.

"Not a problem," he says. "We'll just put some honey on your husband's penis, he can put it back inside you, and the bee will come out when he does."

"Oh no," the husband says. "I'm allergic to bee stings. They could kill me."

"Well . . ." the doctor says. "I guess I could do it."

The couple agree that something has to be done quickly, and soon enough the doctor is applying honey to his penis.

He gingerly inserts the organ into the woman, then suddenly grabs her shoulders and begins humping her vigorously.

"Change of plans," the doctor says. "I'm going to drown the bastard."

❧

Q: WHY DO MEN WEAR JOCKSTRAPS?
A: So they don't get headaches.

An old geezer goes to the doctor asking for a prescription for Viagra. The guy asks for a large dose of maximum strength. The doctor asks why he needs so much. The guy says that two young nymphomaniacs are spending a week at his place. The doctor fills the prescription.

Later that week, the same guy goes back to the doctor asking for painkillers.

"Wow," the doctor says, "your dick hurts that bad, huh?"

"No," the old man replies. "It's for my wrists. The girls never showed up."

Three guys are debating who has the best memory.

The first guy says, "I can remember the first day of my first-grade class."

The second guy says, "I can remember my first day at nursery school!"

The third guy says, "That's nothing. I can remember going to the senior prom with my father, and coming home with my mother!"

Q: WHAT DO WIVES AND TRASH HAVE IN COMMON?
A: It's hard to find a good man to take them out.

Q: WHY DID GOD CREATE MAN?
A: Because a vibrator can't mow the lawn.

A young guy goes into a bar and says to the bartender, "Give me six double vodkas."

The bartender says, "Hey, that's a lot of vodka! What are you celebrating?"

The guy says, "I just had my first blow job."

The bartender says, "Well, in that case, let me buy you a seventh!"

The guy says, "No thanks. If six doubles won't get rid of the taste, I'm sure a seventh won't make any difference."

A man asked his doctor if he thought he'd live to be a hundred.

The doctor asked the man, "Do you smoke or drink?"

"No," he replied, "I've never done either."

"Do you gamble, drive fast motorcycles, or fool around with women?" inquired the doctor.

"No, I've never done any of those things either."

"Well then," said the doctor, "why do you want to live so long?"

Q: WHAT DID THE GUY WHO WON FIRST PLACE IN THE OLYMPICS DO WITH HIS GOLD MEDAL?

A: He had it bronzed.

A guy goes to a doctor and says, "Doc, you've got to help me. My penis is orange." The doctor asks the guy to drop his pants so he can check. Damned if the guy's penis isn't orange. The doctor tells the guy, "This is very strange, although sometimes things like this are caused by stress. How are things going at work?" The guy responds that he was fired about two months ago. The doctor tells him that this could be the cause of the stress.

The man responds, "No. The boss was a real asshole, I had to work twenty to thirty hours of overtime every week, and I had no say in anything that was happening. I found a new job a couple of weeks ago where I can set my own hours, I'm getting paid double what I got on the old job, and the boss is a really great guy."

So the doc figures this isn't the reason. He asks the guy, "How's your life at home?"

The man says, "Well, I got divorced about eight months ago." The doc figures that this has got to be the reason for all of the man's stress, but the man says, "No. For years, all I listened to was nag, nag, nag. God, am I glad to be rid of that old bitch."

So the doc takes a few minutes to think a little longer. He inquires, "Do you have any hobbies or a social life?"

The guy replies, "No, not really. Most nights I sit home, watch some porno flicks, and munch on Chee • tos."

A wealthy woman marries a man with no resources. Over the years, she begins to wonder if her husband married her for her money. One day, she decides to confront him about it.

"Honey, would you have married me even if my father didn't leave me all that money?" she says.

"Of course, dear," he replies. "I wouldn't have cared who left you the money."

Height of competition: a guy peeing beside a waterfall.

🃏

Three bored housewives were chatting over coffee about their love lives.

"I call my husband the dentist because nobody can drill like he does," one woman boasted.

The second woman giggled and confessed, "I call my husband the miner because of his incredible shaft."

The third woman quietly sipped her Jamba Juice, then finally frowned and sighed, "I call my husband the postman. He always delivers late, and half the time it's in the wrong box."

🃏

Q: WHY DO MOST MEN PREFER LOOKS OVER BRAINS?
A: Because most men see better than they think.

🃏

Height of frustration: a boxer trying to scratch his balls.

🃏

A doctor told his patient that her test results indicated that she had a rare disease and had only six months to live.

"Isn't there anything I can do?" pleaded the patient.

"Marry a lawyer," the doctor advised. "It will be the longest six months of your life."

🃏

Husbands are like cars. They're good for the first year.

Two young lovers go up to the mountains for a romantic winter vacation. When they get there, the guy goes out to chop some wood. When he gets back, he says, "Honey, my hands are freezing!"

She says, "Well, put them here between my thighs, and that will warm them up."

After lunch, he goes back out to chop some more wood and comes back and again says, "My hands are really freezing!"

Again, she says, "Well, put them here between my thighs and warm them up." He does, and again that warms him up.

After dinner, he goes out one more time to chop some wood to get them through the night. When he returns, he says again, "Honey, my hands are really, really freezing!"

She looks at him and says, "For crying out loud, don't your ears ever get cold?"

Give a man an inch and he thinks he's a ruler.

The only thing that the IRS has not yet taxed is the male penis. This is due to the fact that 40 percent of the time it is hanging around unemployed, 30 percent of the time it is hard up, 20 percent of the time it is pissed off, and 10 percent of the time it is in the hole. On top of that, it has two dependents and they are both nuts.

A drunk had been drinking at a pub all night. The bartender finally said that the bar was closing, so the drunk stood up to leave and fell flat on his face. He tried to stand one more time same result. He figured he'd crawl outside and get some fresh air and maybe that would sober him up.

Once outside, he stood up and fell flat on his face, so he decided to crawl the four blocks to his home. When he arrived at the door, he stood up and again fell flat on his face. He crawled through the door and into his bedroom.

When he reached his bed, he tried one more time to stand up. This time he managed to pull himself upright, but he quickly fell right into bed and was sound asleep as soon as his head hit the pillow.

He awoke the next morning to his wife standing over him, shouting, "So, you've been out drinking again!"

"What makes you say that?" he asked, putting on an innocent look.

"The pub called. You left your wheelchair there again."

***

God created man first. Then She sobered up.

***

Two men waiting at the Pearly Gates strike up a conversation.

"How'd you die?" the first man asks the second.

"I froze to death," says the second.

"That's awful; how does it feel to freeze to death?" says the first.

"It's very uncomfortable at first; you get the shakes, and you get pains in all your fingers and toes. But eventually it's a very calm way to go. You get numb and you kind of drift off, as if you're sleeping. How did you die?" says the second.

"I had a heart attack," says the first guy. "You see, I knew my wife was cheating on me, so one day I showed up at home unexpectedly. I ran up to the bedroom and found her alone, knitting. I ran down to the basement, but no one was hiding there. I ran up to the second floor, but no one was hiding there either. I ran as fast as I could to the attic, and just as I got there, I had a massive heart attack and died."

The second man shakes his head. "That's too bad," he says. "If you had only stopped to look in the freezer, we'd both still be alive."

Q: WHY DO MEN PAY MORE FOR CAR INSURANCE?
A: Women don't get blow jobs while they're driving.

Two guys are drinking in a bar when one falls backward off his stool and slams hard onto the floor.

"That's one thing about John," the bartender says. "He always knows when to stop."

Q: HOW ARE MEN LIKE VACATIONS?
A: They're never quite long enough.

The grieving widow goes to her local newspaper to submit an obituary. The man behind the counter tells her it will cost five dollars per word.

She thinks for a moment and says, "Fred's dead."

The man then informs her there is a five-word minimum.

She says, "Okay . . . 'Fred's dead; Buick for sale.' "

✳

A man picks up a young woman in a bar and convinces her to come back to his hotel, where they couple passionately.

When they are relaxing afterward, he asks, "Am I the first man you ever made love to?"

She looks at him thoughtfully for a minute.

"You might be," she says. "Your face looks familiar."

Q: WHY DID THE WOMAN WEAR BLACK TO BED?
A: To mourn the dead prick beside her.

A man took his wife to a Broadway show. During the first intermission, he had to pee very badly, so he hurried to find the bathrooms. He searched and searched until he found himself in a dark hall with a beautiful fountain and lots of plants. Since nobody was watching, he decided to relieve himself right there.

When he finally got back into the auditorium, the second act had already begun. He searched in the dark until he found his wife. "Did I miss much of the second act?" he asked.

"Miss it?" she said. "You were in it!"

Q: HOW ARE MEN LIKE BROKEN ELEVATORS?
A: They stink and won't go down.

Two eggs are boiling in a pan, and the first egg says to the other egg, "How can they expect us to get hard in three minutes when we just got laid?"

Q: WHAT DO YOU CALL A WOMAN WHO KNOWS WHERE HER HUSBAND IS EVERY NIGHT?

A: A widow.

Q: WHAT HAPPENED TO THE MAN FROM OUT WEST WHO TRIED OUT FOR THE WATER-POLO TEAM?

A: He drowned his horse.

Q: HOW ARE MEN LIKE MICROWAVES?

A: They heat up instantly and go off in forty-five seconds.

Q: WHY DON'T MEN DRINK COFFEE BEFORE SEX?

A: It keeps them awake.

Q: HOW DID THE REDNECK FIND HIS SISTER IN THE WOODS.

A: Pretty hot.

A young couple were married and celebrated their first night together with lots of sex—a first for both of them. Morning comes and the groom goes into the bathroom but finds no towel when he emerges from the shower. He asks the bride to please bring one from the bedroom. When she gets to the bathroom door, he opens the door, exposing his body for the first time to his bride.

Her eyes go up and down and at about midway, they stop and stare. She asks shyly, "What's that?"

He, also being shy, thinks for a minute and then says, "Well, that's what we had so much fun with last night."

And she, in amazement, asks, "Is that all we have left?"

Q: HOW MANY MEN DOES IT TAKE TO CHANGE A ROLL OF TOILET PAPER?

A: Nobody knows.

Two women are talking at a bar about their concept of the ideal man. Finally, they decide that the ideal man has an eighteen-inch tongue and can breathe through his ears.

Q: WHAT'S THE ONE THING THAT KEEPS MOST MEN OUT OF COLLEGE?

A: High school.

A woman, getting married for the fourth time, goes to a bridal shop and asks for a white dress.

"You can't wear white," says the salesclerk. "You've been married three times already."

"Of course I can—I'm a virgin!" says the bride.

"Impossible," says the salesclerk.

"Unfortunately not," the bride says. "My first husband was a psychologist. All he wanted to do was talk about it. My second husband was a gynecologist. All he wanted to do was look at it. My third husband was a stamp collector. God, I miss him."

Q: WHAT IS THE DEFINITION OF AN INCONSIDERATE HUSBAND?

A: One who wins a trip to Paris and goes by himself, twice.

A man in his eighties gets up, puts on his coat, and tells his wife, "I'm going to the doctor."

"Why?" she asks. "Are you sick?"

"No," he says. "I'm going to get me some of those new Viagra pills."

So his wife gets up out of her rocker and is putting on her sweater when he asks, "Where are you going?"

"I'm going to the doctor, too."

"Why?"

She replies, "If you're going to start using that rusty old thing again, I'm going to get a tetanus shot."

Two men are out fishing and they're having great luck. They are catching fish so fast, they have to leave early.

"This is so great," says the first guy. "We should mark the spot so we can come here again."

"You're right," says the other guy, who dives over the side

and paints a big *X* on the bottom of the boat. Then they head back to shore.

Just as they're about to dock, the first guy looks at the second guy and says, "But what if we don't get the same boat?"

🃏

A mother and daughter are talking about the facts of life.

The girl says, "Mommy, what's a penis?"

Her mother says, "That's what your father pees with."

Then the girl says, "So what's a prick?"

Her mother frowns and says, "That's what is attached to the penis."

🃏

Q: HOW COME JOCKS DON'T GO ELEPHANT HUNTING?

A: They get too tired carrying the decoys.

🃏

Q: WHY CAN'T STEVIE WONDER SORT HIS LAUNDRY?

A: He's a man.

🃏

Q: WHY DID THE JOCK SELL HIS WATER SKIS?

A: He couldn't find a lake on a hill.

🃏

An Irishman was in the south of France and couldn't understand why François had attracted so many girls on the beach and he had attracted no one. So he asked François, "How do you manage to attract all the girls?"

François said, "Take a potato and tuck it in your swim trunks—it drives the women wild."

So the Irishman stuffed a potato in his trunks and paraded up and down the beach. After many hours, however, he still failed to arouse any woman's interest.

So the Irishman went to see François again and said, "I've tried it, François, but it doesn't work!"

François took one look at the Irishman and said, "You might try putting the potato in the front of your bathing suit!"

If a man is alone in the woods without a woman to hear him, is he still wrong?

Q: WHY DO WOMEN HAVE MORE TROUBLE WITH HEMOR-
RHOIDS THAN MEN?
A: Because God made man the perfect asshole.

Men are like campfires. They go out if left unattended.

Two coworkers finally sleep together after flirting for months. The man says, "Since I met you, I've wanted to make love to you in the worst way."

The woman says, "Well, you succeeded."

A guy is returning a chain saw to a hardware store.

"You told me I could cut down ten trees down in an hour with this thing," the customer says. "It took me all day just to cut just one."

The clerk takes the saw, figuring something must be wrong with it. After he starts it, the customer plugs both his ears and starts shouting, "What's that noise?"

The definition of indecent: in deep, in long, and in hard.

Q: HOW ARE HUSBANDS DIFFERENT FROM DOGS?
A: After a year, the dog is still excited to see you.

A man is out in the Chinese wilderness and he's hopelessly lost. It's been nearly three weeks since he's eaten anything besides what he could forage, and he's been reduced to sleeping in caves and under trees. One afternoon, he comes upon an old mansion in the woods. It has vines covering most of it and the man can't see any other buildings in the area. He sees smoke coming out of the chimney, though, which suggests that someone is home.

He knocks on the door and an old man answers, with a beard almost down to the ground. The old man squints his eyes and says, "What do you want?"

The man says "I've been lost for the past three weeks and haven't had a decent meal or sleep in all that time. I would be most grateful if I could have a meal and sleep in your house just for tonight."

The old Chinese man says, "I'll let you come in on one condition—you cannot mess around with my granddaughter."

The man, who is exhausted and hungry, readily agrees, saying, "I promise I won't cause you any trouble. I'll be on my way tomorrow morning."

The old Chinese man says, "Okay, but if I do catch you, then I'll give you the three worst Chinese torture tests ever known to man."

"Okay, okay," the man says as he enters the old house. "Besides," he thinks to himself, "what kind of a woman would live out in the wilderness all her life?"

Well, that evening, the man came down to dinner and saw how beautiful the granddaughter was. Later that night, the man sneaked into the girl's bedroom and they had quite a time, but had kept the noise down to a minimum. The man crept back to his room later, thinking to himself, "Any three torture tests would be worth it after that experience."

The next morning, the man awoke to find a heavy weight on his chest. He opened his eyes and there was this huge rock on his chest. On the rock was a sign saying FIRST CHINESE TORTURE TEST: FIFTY-POUND ROCK ON YOUR CHEST.

"What a lame torture test," the man thought to himself as he got up and walked over to the window. He opened the shutter and threw the rock out. On the back side of the rock was another sign that said SECOND-WORST CHINESE TORTURE TEST—ROCK TIED TO RIGHT TESTICLE.

Thinking fast, the man quickly jumped out the window after the rock. Outside the window was a third sign saying THIRD-WORST CHINESE TORTURE TEST—LEFT TESTICLE TIED TO BEDPOST.

Jim joins a very exclusive nudist colony. On his first day he takes off his clothes and starts wandering around. A gorgeous petite blonde walks by him and the man immediately gets an erection. The woman notices his erection, comes over to him smiling sweetly, and says: "Sir, did you call for me?"

Jim replies: "No, what do you mean?"

She says: "You must be new here; let me explain. It's a rule here that if I give you an erection, it implies you called for me." Smiling, she then leads him to the side of a pool, lies down on a towel, eagerly pulls him to her, and happily lets him have his way with her.

Jim continues exploring the facilities. He enters a sauna, sits down, and farts. Within a few seconds a huge, horribly corpulent, hairy man with a firm erection lumbers out of the steam toward him. The huge man says: "Sir, did you call for me?"

Jim replies: "No, what do you mean?"

The big man says, "You must be new here; it is a rule that when you fart, it implies you called for me." The huge man then spins Jim around, bends him over the bench, and has his way with him.

Jim rushes back to the colony office. He is greeted by the smiling naked receptionist: "May I help you?" she asks.

Jim says, "Here is your card and key back. You can keep the $500 membership fee."

The receptionist says, "But, sir, you've only been here a couple of hours; you only saw a small fraction of our facilities."

Jim replies: "Listen, lady, I am fifty-eight years old, I get a hard-on twice a month, but I fart 15 times a day. No thanks."

Q: WHY DO MEN HAVE DICKS?
A: Because eventually toy cars get boring.

A man phones home from the office and tells his wife, "I have the chance to go hunting for a week. It's the opportunity of a lifetime. We leave right away, so pack my clothes, my gun and ammo box, and my blue silk pajamas. I'll be home in an hour to pick them up." He hurries home, grabs everything, and rushes off.

A week later, he returns. His wife asks, "Did you have a good trip?"

"Oh yes, great! But you forgot to pack my blue silk pajamas."

"Oh no, I didn't. I put them in your ammo box."

A salesman in a strange city was feeling horny and wanted release. He inquired for the address of a good house of ill repute. He was told to go to 225 West North Street. By mistake, he went to 235 West North Street, the office of a podiatrist. Being met by a beautiful woman in a white uniform surprised but intrigued him. She directed him to an examining room and told him to uncover and someone would be with him soon.

He loved the thought of the table and the reclining chair and was really getting aroused because of the strange and different approach this house offered.

Finally, the doctor's assistant, a really gorgeous redhead, entered and found him sitting in the chair with his generous member in his hand.

"My goodness," she exclaimed, "I was expecting to see a foot."

"Well," he said, "if you're going to complain about an inch, then I'll take my business elsewhere."

Q: WHY DIDN'T THE HUSBAND CHANGE THE BABY FOR A WEEK?

A: Because the diaper package said, "22–40 lbs."

Q: IF EVE WORE A FIG LEAF, WHAT DID ADAM WEAR?

A: A hole in the fig leaf.

A man walks into the front door of a bar. He is obviously drunk. He staggers up to the bar, seats himself on a stool, and slurs his drink order to the bartender.

"You're cut off, buddy," the bartender says. "Take a hike." And the bouncer tosses him out the front door.

Five minutes later, the same drunk walks through the side door of the bar, sits down at a stool, and again asks for a drink.

"I already told you, buddy. You're out!" the bartender says as the bouncer tosses the guy right back out the side door.

Ten minutes later, the drunk staggers in through the back door, plops down on a stool, and orders a drink.

"If I see you again," the bartender shouts, "I'm going to call the cops."

And as the bouncer grabs him by the shoulder, the drunk looks up and says, "Jeez. How many bars do you guys work at?"

Q: HOW IS ANTARCTICA LIKE A WOMAN'S CLITORIS?

A: Most men know it's down there, but they don't care.

A woman rushes into her house one morning and yells to her husband, "Sam, pack up your stuff. I just won the lottery!"

"Should I pack for warm weather or cold?"

"Whatever you want. Just so you're out of the house by noon!"

Q: HOW DO YOU TELL IF A MAN IS HAPPY?
A: Why would you?

Q: WHY ARE WOMEN SO BAD AT MATH?
A: Because men keep telling that this [a thumb right by a forefinger] is nine inches.

A Mexican, a Polack, an African-American, an Italian, a priest, a rabbi, and a nun walk into a bar. The bartender looks up and says, "What is this? Some kind of joke?"

A man is screwing his best friend's wife when he suddenly stops and holds his head in his hands.

"I can't believe I'm doing this," he moans. "Getting my best friend's pussy."

"Oh, honey," she says. "This isn't your best friend's pussy. His is three inches deeper."

Two women were making conversation at a cocktail party.

One said to the other, "Aren't you wearing your wedding ring on the wrong finger?"

The other replied, "Yes, I am. I married the wrong man."

🐺

Q: WHAT'S THE DIFFERENCE BETWEEN A MAN AND A CAMEL?

A: A camel can work for eight days without drinking, while a man can drink for eight days without working.

🐺

Nick goes over to his friend's house, rings the bell, and his friend's wife opens the door wearing only a robe.

"Hi, is Bill home?" asks Nick.

"No, he went to the store," replies the wife.

"Well, you mind if I wait?" asks Nick.

"No, come in," responds the wife.

They sit down and Nick says, "You know, you have the greatest breasts I have ever seen. I'll give you a hundred bucks if I can just see one." She thinks about this for a second and figures what the hell, it's a hundred bucks. She opens her robe and shows him one. He thanks her and throws a hundred bucks on the table.

They sit there awhile longer and Nick says, "They are so beautiful, I've got to see both of them. I'll give you another hundred bucks if I can just see both of them together." She thinks about this and decides what the hell, opens her robe, and gives Nick a nice long look. Nick thanks her, throws another hundred bucks on the table, and then says he can't wait any longer and leaves.

A while later Bill arrives home and his wife says, "You know, your friend Nick came over."

Bill thinks about this for a second and says, "Well, did he drop off the $200 he owes me?"

Two women are talking over a cup of coffee.

"Did I tell you I ran into my ex the other day?" said the first.

"No," said the second. "What'd you do?"

"I backed up and ran over him again," said the first.

Q: WHAT DO YOU CALL A DRUNK IN A SUIT?
A: The defendant.

Three guys are going hunting. The first guy comes back that night with a big bear.

"How'd you do that?" the second guy asks.

"I followed the tracks, went in a cave, and shot the bear."

The next night, the second guys comes back, and he, too, has a bear.

"How'd you do that?" the third guys asks.

"I followed the tracks, went in a cave, and shot the bear."

The next night, the third guy crawls back with both legs broken and a bleeding head.

"What happened to you?" the first guy asks.

"I followed the tracks, went in a cave, and then a train hit me."

A guy asks his friend, "If you heard a nuclear missile was coming in 30 minutes, what would you do?"

The man answers, "I'd probably fuck the first thing that moved. What would you do?"

"Stand very still."

A man and a woman started to have sex in the middle of the woods, where it is pitch-black. After about fifteen minutes, the man gets up and says, "Damn, I wish I had a flashlight!"

The woman says, "I wish you did, too. You've been eating grass for the past ten minutes."

A young couple, just married, were in their honeymoon suite on their wedding night. As they undressed for bed, the husband, who was a big, burly man, tossed his pants to his bride and said, "Here; put these on."

She put them on and the waist was twice the size of her body. "I can't wear your pants!" she said.

He shot her a look, paused, and then said, "That's right, and don't you forget it. I'm the one who wears the pants in this family."

Hearing that, she flipped him her panties and said, "Try these on."

He tried them on and found he could only get them as far as his kneecaps. He said, "I can't get into your panties!"

She said, "And that's the way it's going to be until your attitude changes."

Jim stopped at his favorite watering hole after a hard day's work. He noticed a man next to him ordering a shot and a beer. The man drank the shot, chased it with the beer, and then looked into his shirt pocket. This continued several times before Jim's curiosity got the best of him. He leaned over to the guy and said, "Excuse me, I couldn't help but notice your little ritual. Why in the world do you look into your shirt pocket every time you drink your shot and beer?"

The man replied, "There's a picture of my wife in there, and when she starts to look good, then I go home!"

Q: HOW ARE MEN LIKE LAWN MOWERS?
A: If you're not pushing one around, you're riding it.

Q: HOW DOES A MAN SHOP FOR UNDERWEAR?
A: He drops it on the floor to see if it looks good.

Q: WHAT HAS SIX BALLS AND SCREWS REDNECKS?
A: The lottery.

A teacher asks her class, "If there are five blue jays sitting on a fence and you shoot one of them, how many will be left?" Then she calls on Johnny.

"None, they all fly away with the first gunshot."

The teacher replies, "The correct answer is four, but I like your thinking."

Then Johnny says, "I have a question for you. There are

three women sitting on a bench having ice cream. One is delicately licking the sides of the triple scoop of ice cream. The second is gobbling down the top and sucking the cone. The third is biting off the top of the ice cream. Which one is married?"

The teacher, blushing, replies, "Well, I suppose the one that's gobbled down the top and sucked the cone."

"The correct answer is the one with the wedding ring on . . . but I like your thinking."

After the annual office Christmas party, John woke up with a pounding headache, cottonmouth, and utterly unable to recall the events of the preceding evening. After a trip to the bathroom, he was able to make his way downstairs, where his wife put some coffee in front of him. "Louise," he moaned, "tell me what went on last night. Was it as bad as I think?"

"It was awful," she said in her most scornful tone. "You made a complete ass of yourself, succeeded in antagonizing the entire board of directors, and insulted the CEO of the company to his face."

"He's an arrogant, self-important prick," he countered. "Piss on him!"

"Well, that's just what you did. All over his suit," Louise told him. "And he fired you."

"Well, fuck him," said John.

"I did. You're back at work on Monday."

Q: HOW DID THE MAN KNOW HIS ROOMMATE HAD GONE GAY?
A: His dick started to taste like shit.

This guy visits the doctors and says, "Doc, I think I've got a sex problem. I can't get it up for my wife anymore."

The doctor says, "Come back tomorrow and bring her with you." The next day, the guy shows up with his wife.

The doctor says to the wife, "Take off your clothes and lie on the table." She does as he asks, and the doctor walks around the table a few times looking her up and down. Then he pulls the guy to the side and says, "You're fine. She doesn't give me a hard-on, either."

Q: WHAT HAPPENED TO THE MAN WHOSE WIFE MIXED HIS VIAGRA TABLETS WITH SLEEPING PILLS?

A: She found him in his favorite chair having forty wanks.

The husband was furious when he found out that his and his wife's joint checking account was empty. When he confronted his wife, she just said, "It's my turn."

"What do you mean, 'your turn'?" yelled the husband.

"In bed, you've been making early withdrawals for years," she said. "Now it's my turn."

Q: HOW IS A SOFT PENIS LIKE A RATTLESNAKE?

A: You can't fuck with either one.

The bride-to-be, upon her engagement, went to her mother and said, "I've found a man just like father!"

Her mother replied, "So what do you want from me—sympathy?"

A guy went out hunting. He had all the gear: the jacket, the boots and the double-barreled shotgun. As he was climbing over a fence, he dropped the gun and it went off, right near his penis. Obviously, he had to see a doctor. When he woke up from surgery, he found that the doctor had done a marvelous job repairing it.

After he recovered, and as he got ready to go home, the doctor gave him a business card and said, "This is my brother's card. Call and make an appointment to see him."

The guy said, "Is your brother a doctor?"

"No," the doctor replied. "He plays the flute. He'll show you where to put your fingers so you don't piss in your eye."

Q: DID YOU HEAR ABOUT THE MADAM WHO COULDN'T SPELL?
A: She bought a warehouse.

Q: WHAT IS A MAN'S IDEA OF SAFE SEX?
A: A padded headboard.

Q: DID YOU HEAR ABOUT THE BABY BORN AS BOTH A BOY AND A GIRL?

A: The baby had both a penis *and* a brain.

🐾

A professor of mathematics left this letter on the kitchen counter:

Dear Wife,

You must realize that you are fifty-four years old, and I have certain needs which you are no longer able to satisfy. I am otherwise happy with you as a wife, and I sincerely hope you will not be hurt or offended to learn that by the time you receive this letter, I will be at the Hilton Hotel with my eighteen-year-old teaching assistant. I'll be home before midnight.

Your Husband

When he arrived at the hotel, there was a faxed letter waiting for him that read as follows:

Dear Husband,

You, too, are fifty-four years old, and by the time you receive this letter, I will be at the Sheraton Hotel with the eighteen-year-old pool boy. Since you are a mathematician, you will appreciate that eighteen goes into fifty-four more times than fifty-four goes into eighteen. Therefore, don't wait up.

Your Wife

🐾

Q: WHAT DO BOYFRIENDS AND BOWLING BALLS HAVE IN COMMON?
A: Both tend to land in the gutter.

❧

Q: WHY AREN'T THERE MANY MALE PHARMACISTS?
A: They can't figure out how to get the pill bottles into the typewriter.

❧

A man on his deathbed knew he had seen his last sunrise. Lying there, he suddenly detected the scent of his favorite dessert: chocolate chip cookies. He couldn't resist the smell, so he struggled out of his bed and into his robe. Then, with the last ounce of his strength, he hugged the wall of his room, then slumped on the banister and heaved himself down, step by painful step. He shuffled into the kitchen and saw the cookies cooling on the rack—just where his wife had always left them.

As the old man reached for the largest cookie on the tray, a spatula slapped him on the hand.

"Don't touch those!" his wife barked. "They're for the funeral."

❧

Three guys leave their wives for a weekend in Las Vegas, and they promptly head for a brothel. There's only one woman available, so they agree to take turns.

The first one comes back and says, "She was good, but my wife is better."

The second one comes back and says, "She was definitely good, but my wife is better."

The third one comes back and says, "You're both right."

Behind every great man is a puzzled woman.

※

This woman goes into a sporting-goods store to buy a rifle.

"It's for my husband," she tells the assistant.

"Did he tell you what gauge to get?" asks the assistant.

"Are you joking?" she says. "He doesn't even know I'm going to shoot him."

※

A man turned 105 and was being interviewed by a reporter for the local paper. During the interview at the man's house, the reporter noticed that the yard was full of children of all ages playing together. A very pretty girl of about nineteen served the old man and the reporter, keeping their iced-tea glasses full.

"Are these your grandkids?" the reporter asked.

"They're all my children," the old man replied with a grin.

"Your kids?" asked the reporter. "What about this beautiful young lady who keeps bringing us iced tea? Is she one of your children, too?"

"No, sir," said the old man. "She's my wife."

"Your wife?" said the surprised reporter. "But she can't be more than nineteen years old."

"That's right," said the old man with pride.

"Well, how on earth can you satisfy that young woman at your age?" the startled reporter asked.

"We have sex every night," the old man said. "Every night two of my boys help me on her, and every morning six of my boys help me off."

"Wait just one minute," said the newspaperman. "Why

does it only take two of your boys to put you on, but it takes six of them to take you off?"

"Because," the old man said with a clenched fist, "I fights 'em."

Q: HOW DO YOU GET A GOOD-LOOKING GUY'S EYES TO LIGHT UP?
A: Shine a flashlight in his ear.

A guy sees his new neighbor out in his backyard, so he decides to get acquainted. After introductions, he asks the new neighbor what he does for a living.

The new neighbor says, "I'm a professor of logic."

"What's that?" the guy asks.

"Well, let me see if I can explain logic to you." The professor scans the backyard, and spies an empty doghouse. "You have a dog, correct?"

"Well, yeah, I do!"

"I thought so," the professor says. Eyeing the swing set, he says: "And you have children, too?"

"I sure do!"

Then the professor sees a clothesline with women's underwear. "And a wife?"

"Sure!"

"And you are also heterosexual."

"I am!"

The professor clears his throat. "You see, I saw a doghouse, a swing set, and a bra hanging on a clothesline. Logic would suggest you have a dog, children, and a wife, which would also indicate that you are heterosexual."

"Wow!" the guys says. The next day he is talking to a

friend who asks about the new neighbor. The friend, too, is a bit confused about logic.

"Let me see if I can explain it," the guy says. "Do you have a doghouse in your yard?"

"No," the friend says.

"Then you're gay."

<hr/>

Q: WHAT'S HARD AND PINK WHEN IT GOES IN, AND WARM AND SOFT WHEN IT COMES OUT?

A: Bubble gum.

<hr/>

Q: HOW ARE A MARRIAGE AND A TORNADO ALIKE?

A: At first, there's a lot of sucking and blowing, and at the end, you lose your house.

<hr/>

A young woman creeps out of bed, leaving her elderly husband there to snore. She walks out into the hall and grabs her stepson for a little fling.

"I can't go in there!" the young man protests. "My dad will wake up."

"Don't be silly," she says, yanking a hair from the old man's ass. "Nothing wakes him up from a deep sleep."

So the two start going at it, and she lets out a loud moan. "Shhhh!" the young man says, but she yanks another hair out and says, "See."

So they're back at it, and the woman gets so turned on, she starts kicking her husband.

"Careful," the young man says.

But she pulls out another hair, and her husband mutters,

"Look, I don't care if you fuck my son. Just don't use my ass as a scoreboard."

※

One woman we know described her husband as so thick, it takes him two hours to watch *60 Minutes*.

※

A married couple went to the hospital to have their baby delivered. Upon their arrival, the doctor said he had invented a new machine that would transfer a portion of the mother's labor pains to the father.

He asked if they were willing to try it out. Since the woman was afraid of pain, and since her husband very much wanted to help her, they both said yes. The doctor set the pain transfer to 10 percent for starters, explaining that even 10 percent was probably more pain than the father had ever experienced before. But as the labor progressed, the husband felt fine and asked the doctor to go ahead and kick it up a notch. The doctor then adjusted the machine to 20 percent pain transfer. The husband was still feeling fine.

The doctor checked the husband's blood pressure and was amazed at how well he was doing. At this point, they decided to try for 50 percent. The husband continued to feel quite well. Since the pain transfer was obviously helping the wife out considerably, and since he loved her very much, the husband encouraged the doctor to transfer *all* the pain to him. The wife delivered a healthy baby with virtually no pain. She and her husband were ecstatic.

When they got home, the mailman was dead on the porch.

※

Luke and Betty-Sue get married, and Luke whisks her away to his daddy's hunting cabin in the woods for a romantic "nature honeymoon."

He carries her across the threshold, and they get into bed, when Betty-Sue whispers in his ear, "Luke, be gentle, I ain't never been with a man b'fore."

"WHAT?" shouts Luke, and his little bride softly shakes her head.

Luke jumps out of bed, grabs his clothes, and races out the door, into his truck . . . down the mountain . . . straight to his parents' house.

He rushes inside screaming, "Hey, Daddy! Paw! Git up!"

His father rushes downstairs and gasps, "Luke, whatcha you doin' here?"

Luke, still breathing hard from his mad flight, manages to say, "Well, Betty-Sue an' I was in the cabin, and she tol' me she ain't never been with a man afore. So's I rushed outta there, an' lit back here, quick as I could!"

His father grasps Luke's shoulder in reassurance, and says, "Son, ya done the right thing. If'in she ain't good 'nuff fer her family, she shure as shit ain't good 'nuff fer ours!"

Three American executives were touring an Arab country when they found themselves in a crowded bazaar. Taking in the sites, they saw a woman walk past a man and his camel. The woman asked what time it was, and the man pulled the beast's testicles and answered: "Seventeen past two."

The men looked at their digital watches and found that the camel driver was exactly right. They waited a bit, then one went and asked the man for the time. The man pulled his camel's balls and answered: "Twenty-two until three."

Right again!

The second executive repeated the request, and again, the man was right.

Finally, the third executive approached the Arab with five hundred-dollar bills. "I'll pay you this if you can tell me how to tell time like that."

The Arab thought about it, then nodded and took the bills. He motioned for the American to stand by him, crouch a little below the camel's hindquarters, and reach out his hand to palm the camel's testicles.

"Lift the balls very gently," the Arab said, "and look at that clock on the wall over there."

⸎

Q: HOW CAN YOU TELL IF YOU'RE BOYFRIEND IS DUMB?
A: He tries to figure out the best wine to go with his beer.

⸎

A couple of men in a pickup truck drove into a lumberyard. One got out to speak to the clerk in charge.

"We need some four-by-twos," he said.

The clerk said, "You mean two-by-fours, don't you?"

The man said, "I'll go check," and went back to the truck.

He returned a minute later and said, "Yeah, I meant two-by-fours."

"All right. How long do you need them?"

The customer paused for a minute and said, "Uh . . . I'd better go check."

After a while, he returned to the office and said, "A long time. We're gonna build a house."

⸎

A nun in a habit hops in a cab, and the driver can't stop smiling.

"What's so funny, son?"

"Well, Sister, it's embarrassing, but I've always had this fantasy of getting a blow job from a nun."

The nun looks down for a moment, then looks up and says: "I admit I am tempted. But only if you are Christian and not married."

The cabbie answers that he is Christian and not married, and they proceed with their encounter. Afterward, the cabbie feels guilty and blurts out: "Sister, I'm sorry. I lied. I'm married, and I'm Jewish!"

The nun looks down again and says quietly: "It's all right, son. I'm Lutheran and my name is Ralph."

An Italian mother is making spaghetti sauce when she accidentally spills a box of BBs that were on the kitchen counter into the pots. She fishes them out, and decides she doesn't want to start over. So she pours the sauce over the noodles and sits down to dinner with her children.

Two days later, her daughter runs up to her. "Mama, you wouldn't believe it. I just pooped and there was a BB in there!"

"Don't worry, dear, it will pass."

That afternoon, her other daughter comes to her with the same story.

"Don't worry, dear, it will pass."

Late that night, her son comes running up to her, looking very distressed.

"Mama, you won't believe—"

"I know, son. You pooped and there was a BB in there."

"No," he said. "I was whacking off, and I shot the dog."

A man in his forties wearing a stovepipe hat, a waistcoat, and a phony beard sat down at a bar and ordered a drink. As the bartender set it down, he asked, "Going to a costume party?"

"Yeah," the man answered, "I'm supposed to come dressed as my love life."

"But you look like Abe Lincoln!" said the surprised barman.

"That's right. My last four scores were seven years ago."

There's an elegant brass plaque by the door of the fanciest house of prostitution in town. It says: IT'S A BUSINESS DOING PLEASURE WITH YOU.

At their buddy's wedding reception, three pals—a plumber, a carpenter, and a dentist—agreed they needed some pranks to play on the wedding night. The plumber said he would turn off the hot water in the honeymoon suite. The carpenter said he would saw off the slats in the bed. The dentist just smiled.

A few days later, each got a letter:

Dear Friends:

When we had to take a cold shower together, we were sort of thrilled. And the bed falling apart made us laugh. But if we catch the son of a bitch who put Novocain in the Vaseline . . .

After far too many drinks, a man down on his luck staggers into a church and plunks himself down in a confessional. After a few minutes of listening to the man moaning, a priest steps into the adjoining booth.

"Son, may I help you?" he asks through the screen.

"God, I hope so," the man replies. "Do you have any toilet paper in that one?"

A young couple got married, and in their family, it was a tradition that the groom's brother dance with the bride for the first song. So they did. But then they danced for the second song, too. And the third. By the time the fourth song began, the groom ran up and kicked the bride between the legs. A huge fight broke out, and the wedding party and all the guests were hauled off to jail. In court the next week, the judge asked the brother what happened.

"Your Honor, we were just dancing, and the groom ran up and kicked the bride between the legs."

"That must have hurt," said the judge.

"No kidding," said the brother. "He broke three of my fingers."

Mark, Jed, and Michael visit a prostitute, who agrees to give them a deal. "You can each pay by the inch."

Mark comes out and announces he got a bill for seventy-five dollars.

Then Jed walks out, and says it cost him ninety dollars.

Finally, out comes Michael.

"She charged me thirty dollars," he says, and the other two guys start to laugh.

"Look, I'm not stupid," Michael says. "I'm the only one who paid on the way out instead of the way in."

***

Q: HOW CAN YOU TELL A BACHELOR FROM A MARRIED MAN?
A: A bachelor comes to work each morning from a different direction.

***

A man sticks his head into a barbershop looking for a friend: "Bob Peters in here?"

"Nope," the man in the first chair said. "Just haircuts and shaves."

***

Q: WHY IS A GINGERBREAD MAN BETTER THAN A REAL MAN?
A: He's sweet, he listens, and if you get mad, you can bite his head off.

***

The bartender was washing his glasses when an elderly Irishman came in. With great difficulty, the Irishman hoisted his bad knee over a bar stool, pulled himself up painfully, and asked for a sip of Irish whiskey.

The Irishman looked down the bar and asked, "Is that Jesus down there?"

The bartender nodded, so the Irishman told him to give Jesus an Irish whiskey, too.

The next patron to come in was an ailing Italian with a

hunched back, who moved very slowly. He shuffled up to the bar stool and asked for a glass of Chianti.

He also looked down the bar and asked, "Is that Jesus sitting at the end of the bar?"

The bartender nodded, so the Italian said he, too, wanted to give Him a glass of Chianti.

The third patron to enter was a redneck, who swaggered into the bar and hollered, "Barkeep, set me up a cold one!

"Hey, is that God's Boy down there?"

The barkeep nodded, so the redneck told him to give Jesus a cold one, too.

As Jesus got up to leave, he walked over to the Irishman and touched him and said, "For your kindness, you are healed!"

The Irishman felt the strength come back to his leg, so he got up and danced a jig out the door.

Jesus touched the Italian and said, "For your kindness, you are healed!"

The Italian felt his back straighten, so he raised his hands above his head and did a flip out the door.

Jesus walked toward the redneck, but the redneck jumped back and exclaimed, "Don't touch me! I'm drawing disability!"

🕮

Q: WHO WINS TOP MALE OF THE YEAR AWARD?
A: The guy who finishes first in a masturbation race—and third, too.

🕮

A seventy-five-year-old man goes to his doctor complaining about impotence.

"I have an eighty-year-old friend," the man said, "who says he gets it up every night and fucks his nurse."

"Well, sir," the doctor replied. "You can say that, too."

Phillip was on a cruise ship that sank without a trace and found himself the only survivor along with six gorgeous women. They landed on a desert island and quickly made an arrangement. Each woman would have him one night a week, with Sundays being a day of rest.

Phillip loved it, at first even working on his day off. But as the months stretched to years, he began to tire more easily and soon found himself actually looking forward to the day of rest. He even started wishing for another man to take some of the load. One day, another guy *did* wash up on the beach.

Phillip rushed up to him and said, "You have no idea how happy I am to see you."

"Thanks, handsome," the other guy said. "You're looking good yourself."

"Shit," said Phillip. "There go my Sundays."

An Irishman walks into a pub. The bartender asks him, "What'll you have?"

The man says, "Give me three pints of Guinness, please."

So the bartender brings him three pints and the man proceeds to sip one, then the other, then the third until they're gone.

He then orders three more.

The bartender says, "Sir, I know you like them cold. You don't have to order three at a time. I can keep an eye on your drink, and when you get low, I'll bring you a fresh cold one."

The man says, "You don't understand. I have two brothers,

one in Australia and one in the States. We made a vow to each other that every Saturday night we'd still drink together. So right now my brothers have three Guinness stouts, too, and we're drinking together." The bartender thought that was a wonderful tradition.

Every week, the man did the same thing; he came in and ordered three beers.

Then one week he came in and ordered only two. He drank them and then ordered two more.

The bartender said to him, "I know what your tradition is, and I'd just like to say that I'm sorry that one of your brothers died."

The man look puzzled, then his eyes widened.

"Oh, my brothers are fine," he said. "I just quit drinking."

A biology teacher was leading a discussion on reproduction. "Johnny," she asked, "what is the most important part about a mother's milk?"

"It comes in beautiful containers."

One night a man decides to visit his local bar. He takes a seat and orders a beer. After polishing off his beer, he beckons the bartender over and says, "Betcha twenty bucks I can bite my eye." The bartender scoffs and accepts. The man then calmly removes his false eye and bites it. The bartender grudgingly forks over a twenty.

Later that night, after a few more beers, the man wanders back to the bar and says rather drunkenly, "Hey, barkeep, betcha another twenty I can bite my other eye." Wanting to win back his money and seriously doubtful that the man has two false eyes, the bartender accepts. The man calmly removes his false teeth and bites his other eye. Scowling, the bartender hands over another twenty. The man gets up off his bar stool and wanders around as he drinks a few more beers.

He strolls back over to the bar and calls the bartender. "Hey, barkeep," he burbles, "I'll give you a chance to win yer money back plus. Betcha a hundred bucks if you put a shot glass on that end of the bar, and I stand on this end, I can piss into it and not spill a drop."

The bartender eagerly accepts, knowing the feat to be impossible. The man staggers atop the bar, drops a hundred-dollar bill, zips down his fly, and promptly pisses all over the bar.

The bartender pumps his fist in the air and snatches the hundred from the damp bar. The man zips up and is laughing.

"What's so funny?" says the barkeep. "You just lost everything you won and more!"

"Well," giggles the man, "I just bet those guys over there $200 that I could piss all over your bar and you wouldn't get angry."

⛨

Q: WHY IS THERE A HOLE AT THE END OF THE PENIS?
A: So men can get oxygen to their brains.

⛨

If men had periods, they'd brag about the size of their tampons.

⛨

Q: WHY WAS MOSES WANDERING THROUGH THE DESERT FOR FORTY YEARS?
A: Because men refuse to ask for directions!

A man and a woman were having drinks when they got into an argument about who enjoyed sex more. The man said, "Men obviously enjoy sex more than women. Why do you think we're so obsessed with getting laid?"

"That doesn't prove anything," the woman countered. "Think about this . . . when your ear itches and you put your finger in it and wiggle it around, then pull it out, which feels better—your ear or your finger?"

A man and his young son are on their way to go fishing when they stop at a convenience store. The father buys a pack of smokes and a six-pack of beer for himself and a candy bar for his kid.

"Dad, when can I smoke like you?"

"When your wiener is long enough to touch your ass."

"But when can I drink like you?"

"When your wiener is long enough to touch your ass."

So the boy returns to his candy bar, then finds he's got the lucky wrapper. "Dad! It says, 'You Win $1,000,000!' "

"We're rich," the father screams.

"Dad, your wiener is long enough to touch your ass, isn't it?"

"Of course it is!"

"Good," the boy says. "Go fuck yourself."

Bob was in the hospital for a complete checkup. At 11:00 A.M., they brought him soup for lunch. He refused it. At 2:00 P.M., they again tried to serve him some soup, which he again refused.

Again, at 5:00 P.M. and 7:00 P.M., they tried, and both times Bob said he just wasn't hungry. In preparation for the next day's test, they entered his room at 3:00 A.M., 4:30 A.M., and 6:00 A.M. and gave him an enema each time.

When Bob got home from the hospital after the tests, he told his wife, "Whatever you do, if you go to that hospital and they try to serve you soup, take it! If you refuse it, they sneak in while you're asleep and shove it up your butt!"

🔱

A drunk is stumbling down the sidewalk with one foot off the curb. A policeman walks by.

"Buddy, I'm taking you in," the officer says. "You're drunk."

"You think I'm drunk?" the man slurs.

"Yep," the officer replies.

"Oh, good," he says. "I thought I was crippled."

🔱

There was a guy riding through the desert on his camel. He had been traveling so long that he felt the need to have sex. Since there were no women in the desert, the man turned to his camel.

He tried to position himself to have sex with his camel, but the camel ran away. The man ran to catch up to the animal and got back on and started to ride again. Soon he was feeling the urge to have sex again, so once again he turned to his camel. Again the camel refused by running away. So he caught up to it again and got on it again.

Finally, after riding through the desert, the man came to a road. There was a broken-down car with three beautiful women sitting in it. He went up to them and asked if they needed any help.

The hottest girl said, "If you fix our car, we will do anything you want."

The man luckily knew a thing or two about cars and fixed it in a flash. When he finished, one of the girls asked, "How could we ever repay you, mister?"

He thought for a minute. "I've got an idea," he said to the women. "Can you hold my camel?"

⚉

Q: HOW ARE MEN AND WALL-TO-WALL CARPETING SIMILAR?
A: You can walk all over them for life if you lay them right the first time.

⚉

A man sits down at a bar and sees another man at the far end with a miniature piano in front of him. The first man looks closer and realizes there is a tiny man—no taller than a foot—sitting at the piano, tickling the keys. He asks the bartender: "Where in the hell did that come from?"

"There's a genie out back," the bartender answers. "He grants wishes."

"You're kidding!" the man says, starting for the back door.

Sure enough, there's a genie there, who says, "What wish may I grant, sir?"

"I wish I had a million bucks," the man says immediately.

In an instant, flock upon flock of ducks materialize from the walls, swarm the man, and shit hundreds of pounds of duck poop all over his suit.

Terrified, disgusted, the man rushes back into the bar. "Why didn't you tell me that genie was hard-of-hearing?!" he cries.

The man with the little musician looks up and says, "You didn't really think I asked for a twelve-inch pianist, did you?"

A woman was discussing her upcoming wedding night with a friend.

"If you want a great night," the friend said, "get him to slurp a dozen oysters before you go to bed."

Back from the honeymoon, the bride looked a little disappointed.

"Didn't the oysters work," the friend asked.

"Only eight of them!" the bride complained.

On the first day of college, the dean addressed the students, pointing out some of the rules: "The female dormitory will be out-of-bounds for all male students, and the male dormitory to the female students. Anybody caught breaking this rule will be fined $20 the first time." He continued, "Anybody caught breaking this rule the second time will be fined $60. Being caught a third time will cost you a fine of $180. Are there any questions?"

At this point, a male student in the crowd inquired: "How much for a season pass?"

Q: WHAT DO DISNEY WORLD AND VIAGRA HAVE IN COMMON?

A: They both make you wait an hour for a two-minute ride!

Q: WHY DO MEN HAVE TROUBLE MAKING EYE CONTACT WITH WOMEN?

A: Breasts don't have eyes.

An office manager arrives at his department and sees an employee sitting behind his desk totally stressed out. He gives him some advice: "When I thought work was consuming me, I went home every afternoon for two weeks and had myself pampered by my wife. It was fantastic and it really helped; you should try it, too."

Two weeks later, when the manager arrives at his department, he sees the man happy and full of energy at his desk. The faxes are piling up and the computer is running at full speed. He says, "I see you followed my advice."

"I did," answers the employee. "It was great! By the way, I didn't know you had such a nice house!"

A man is at work one day when he notices that his coworker is wearing a tiny diamond stud in his left ear. This man knows his coworker to be a somewhat conservative fellow, so the sudden change in look surprises him. The man walks up to his coworker and says, "I didn't know you were into earrings."

"Don't make such a big deal, it's only an earring," the other man replies sheepishly.

"Well, I'm curious," the man persisted. "How long have you been wearing an earring?"

"Ever since my wife found it in our bed."

Q: HOW ARE MEN LIKE COMPUTERS?
A: You don't appreciate either until they go down on you.

A man is out shopping and discovers a new brand of condoms called Olympic. Thinking to impress his wife, he buys a pack. Upon getting home, he tells her about the purchase he just made.

"Olympic condoms?" she says. "What makes them so special?"

"There are three colors," he replies. "Gold, silver, and bronze."

"What color are you going to wear tonight?" she asks.

"Gold, of course," says the man proudly.

The wife responds, "Why don't you wear silver. It would be nice if you finished second for a change."

Q: WHAT DID THE WIFE OF THE BANKING EXECUTIVE SAY WAS HER ELEVENTH COMMANDMENT?

A: Thou shall not use thy rod on thy staff.

Three men are sitting at a bar. Each says he thinks his wife has been unfaithful.

"I found a hammer and saw under my bed the other day. I think my wife is sleeping with a carpenter."

"I found a helmet and a rubber boot under my bed. I think my wife is sleeping with a fireman."

"That's nothing," the third man says. "Yesterday afternoon, I came home and found a cowboy under my bed. I think my wife is fucking a horse."

A jock walks into the college library and says to the librarian, "Can I have a burger and fries?"

"Sorry," she replies, "this is a library."

So the guy lowers his voice and whispers, "Oh, may I have a burger and fries?"

A man is driving his girlfriend back to his place when she insists he take her home instead. His apartment is so close to the restaurant they just left that he refuses. Then she offers to strip in the car if she'll just take him home. He agrees.

Just as she pulls off her panties, the distracted boyfriend drives the car into a ditch and flips it over. Pinned under the steering wheel, he tells his girlfriend to run and get help.

"But I'm naked!" she says.

"Just take my shoe and cover yourself, and GO!"

She agrees and runs to a nearby house, with only a lone shoe covering her privates. "Please help me! My boyfriend is stuck!"

The man at the front door frowns and says, "I better get a crowbar—I think he's too far in."

Men snore, belch, and pass gas. Women don't, so they have to bitch to keep from exploding.

As a painless way to save money, a young couple arranged that every time they had sex the husband would put his pocket change into a china piggy bank on the bedside table. One night while being unusually athletic, he accidentally knocked the piggy bank onto the floor, where it smashed.

To his surprise, among the masses of coins, there were handfuls of five- and ten-dollar bills. He asked his wife "What's up with all the bills?"

His wife answered: "Not everyone is as cheap as you are."

A guy gets home early from work and hears strange noises coming from the bedroom. He rushes upstairs to find his wife naked on the bed, sweating and panting.

"What's up?" he asks.

"I'm having a heart attack!" cries the woman.

He rushes downstairs to grab the phone, but just as he is dialing, his four-year-old son comes up and says, "Daddy! Daddy! Uncle Dave's hiding in your closet and he's got no clothes on!"

The guy slams the phone down and storms upstairs into the bedroom, past his screaming wife, and rips open the closet door. Sure enough, there is his brother, totally naked, cowering on the floor.

"You bastard," says the husband. "My wife is having a heart attack and you're running around with no clothes on scaring the kids!"

Q: WHY DON'T WOMEN BLINK DURING FOREPLAY?
A: There's not enough time.

A woman's point of view: "Men are like Bordeaux grapes. It's our job to stomp on them and keep them in the dark until they mature into something you'd like to have dinner with."

Sex for men is like banking. First he makes a deposit, then he makes a withdrawal. Then he loses interest.

Q: HOW MANY MEN DOES IT TAKE TO SCREW IN A LIGHT-BULB?

A: Five. One to screw it, four to hear him brag about it.

This guy decides to join the navy. On his first day of service, he gets acquainted with all the facilities around the ship he will be serving on. The guy asks the sailor showing him around, "What do you guys do around here when you get really horny after months of being out at sea?"

The sailor replies, "Well, there is this barrel on the upper deck; just pump your cock in the side with the hole."

Weeks pass, and the new guy is getting real horny and remembers the barrel. He climbs to the upper deck and sees it. He flings his cock out and starts fucking the barrel. It's simply the best feeling he's ever experienced, better than he ever imagined something like that could be.

After he was done, zipped up, and merrily walking along, the sailor who originally told him about the barrel walks by. "That barrel really was great! I could do it every day!" the guy says to him.

To which the sailor replies, "Yeah, you can do it every day except Thursday."

Confused, the new guy asks why, to which the other guy replies, "Because it's your turn in the barrel on Thursday."

Jeff walks into a rest room in an airport and goes up to a urinal. A man with no arms comes up to him and says, "Hey, can you give me a hand?" Though he feels uncomfortable, he agrees to help. He unzips the man's pants, takes a deep breath, and reaches in and takes out his penis, which he is horrified to discover is all green and moldy.

Still feeling pity, he continues to hold the man's penis until he is finished peeing, then gives it a shake and returns it to his pants.

"Hey, thanks a lot, man," the man with no arms says.

"No problem. But there is one thing I have to know. What is wrong with your johnson?"

Then the man pulls out the arms he has been concealing in his sleeves and says, "I don't know, but I'm sure as hell not gonna touch it!"

Q: WHY DOES IT TAKE TWO MILLION SPERM TO FERTILIZE A SINGLE EGG?

A: None of them will stop to ask for directions.

A married woman who was having an affair had her boyfriend over while her husband was out. She left him on the sofa when the phone rang, and was back a few minutes later.

"Who was it?" he asked her.

"My husband," she replied.

"I better get going," he said. "Where is he?"

"Relax. He's downtown playing poker with you."

A blind man was walking down the street with his dog. They stopped at the corner to wait for the passing traffic. The dog started pissing on the man's leg. As the dog finished, the man reached into his coat pocket and pulled out a doggie treat and started waving it at the dog. A passerby saw all the events happening and was shocked. He approached the blind man and said, "I'm not sure if you know this, but that dog just urinated on your leg. You shouldn't be rewarding him."

The blind man replied, "I'm not rewarding him. I'm just trying to find where his head is so I can kick him in the ass."

Q: WHY DO MOST MEN LIKE WOMEN WITH BIG BREASTS AND SMALL VAGINAS?

A: Because most men have big mouths and small dicks.

A man's wife asks him to go to the store to buy some cigarettes. He walks down to the store only to find it closed. So he goes into a nearby bar to use the vending machine. At the bar he sees a beautiful woman and starts talking to her. They have a couple of beers and one thing leads to another and they end up in her apartment.

After they've had their fun, he realizes it's 3:00 A.M. and says, "Oh no, it's so late, my wife's going to kill me. Have you got any talcum powder?" She gives him some talcum powder, which he proceeds to rub on his hands and then he goes home. His wife is waiting for him in the doorway and she is pretty pissed.

"Where the hell have you been!" she screams.

"Well, honey, it's like this," he tells her. "I went to the store, but they were closed. So I went to the bar to use the vending machine. I saw this great-looking chick there and we had a few drinks and one thing led to another and I ended up in bed with her."

"Oh yeah? Let me see your hands!" his wife says. She looks at his hands, which are covered with powder, and says, "Liar! You went bowling again!"

❁

Q: A PERFECT MAN, A PERFECT WOMAN, AND SANTA CLAUS ARE LEAVING A DEPARTMENT STORE. WHO IS HOLDING OPEN THE DOOR?
A: The perfect woman, of course. The other two don't exist.

❁

A doctor walked into a bank. Preparing to endorse a check, he pulled a rectal thermometer out of his shirt pocket and tried to "write" with it. Realizing his mistake, he looked at the thermometer with annoyance and said, "Well, that's great, just great. Some asshole's got my pen."

❁

The woman applying for a job in a Florida lemon grove didn't seem right for the job.

"Listen," said the foreman. "Have you any actual experience in picking lemons?"

"Yes, as a matter of fact I do," she replied. "I've been divorced three times."

❁

Q: WHY DO REDNECKS WEAR JEANS WITH BUTTON FLIES?

A: Sheep can hear a zipper from half a mile away.

When a woman steals your husband, there is no better revenge than to let her keep him.

Two dwarfs decide to treat themselves to a vacation in New Orleans. At the hotel bar, they're dazzled by two women, and wind up taking them to their separate rooms.

The first dwarf is disappointed, however, as he's unable to become aroused enough to have sex with his date. His depression is enhanced by the fact that, from the next room, he hears cries of "ONE, TWO, THREE . . . HUH!" all night long.

In the morning, the second dwarf asks the first, "How did it go?"

The first says, "It was so embarrassing. I couldn't get an erection."

The second dwarf shakes his head. "You think that's embarrassing?" he asks. "I couldn't even get on the bed!"

A man who is not sure he can make his wife come says to her, "Why can't I tell when you have an orgasm?"

"Because you're never here when it happens," she replies.

Q: WHAT DO YOU HAVE WHEN YOU HAVE TWO LITTLE BALLS IN YOUR HAND?

A: A man's undivided attention.

A guy is sitting at a bar in a skyscraper restaurant high above the city. He's slamming tequila left and right. He grabs one, drinks it, goes over to a window, and jumps out. The guy who has been sitting next to him can't believe what he's just seen. He's more surprised when, ten minutes later, the same guy, unscathed, comes walking back into the bar and sits back down next to him.

The astonished guy asks, "How did you do that? I just saw you jump out that window and we're hundreds of feet above the GROUND!"

The jumper responds by slurring, "Well, I don't get it either. I slam a shot of tequila, and when I jump out the window, the tequila makes me slow down right before I hit the ground. Watch."

He takes a shot, slams it down, goes to the window, and jumps out. The other guy runs to the window and watches as the guy falls until, right before the ground, he slows down and lands softly on his feet.

A few minutes later, the guy walks back into the bar. The other guy has to try it, too, so he orders a shot of tequila. He drinks it and goes to the window and jumps. As he reaches the bottom, he doesn't slow down at all . . . *splat!* The first guy orders another shot of tequila and the bartender says to him, "You know, you're really an asshole when you're drunk, Superman."

A young couple sits down for their first session of marriage counseling.

"What seems to be the problem?" the counselor asks.

The wife begins a twenty-minute monologue on the lack of

espect in their marriage, her husband's self-centeredness, his nability to sense or understand her needs, his inattention, and he general malaise that's settled over their sex life.

The counselor walks over, grabs her by the shoulders, and kisses her passionately for two minutes.

"That," he says when finished, "is what your wife needs twice a week."

"Okay," the husband says. "I can have her here on Mondays and Thursdays."

A new bride went to her doctor for a checkup. Lacking any significant knowledge of male anatomy, she asked the doctor, "What's that thing hanging between my husband's legs?"

The doctor replies, "We call that the penis."

The new bride then asks, "What's that reddish-purple thing on the end of the penis?"

The doctor says, "We call that the head of the penis."

She then asks, "What are those two round things about fifteen inches from the head of the penis?"

The doctor replies, "Lady, on him I don't know, but on me they're my ass cheeks!"

A ninety-two-year-old man went to the doctor to get a physical. A few days later, the doctor saw the man walking down the street with a gorgeous young lady on his arm. At his follow-up visit, he said to the man, "You're really doing great, aren't you?"

The man replied, "Just doing what you said, Doctor, 'Get a hot mama and be cheerful.' "

The doctor said, "I didn't say that. I said, 'You got a heart murmur. Be careful.' "

A man walks into a bar and asks for three plums.

The bartender stares at him and says, "We don't serve plums in here."

The man leaves, but comes back the next day and asks for three plums.

"I told you yesterday. We don't have any plums."

The man leaves, but is back the next day with the same request.

"NO PLUMS!" the bartender yells.

The next day, the man is back yet again. "I'd like three plums, please."

Now the bartender loses it. "The next time you ask for plums, I'm going to nail your hand to this bar."

The man looks confused, but leaves. He comes in the next day and says, "I'd like to buy some nails."

The bartender sighs and says, "This is a bar. We don't have any nails."

"In that case," the man says, "I'll take some plums."

A man recently moved to a nudist colony, but decided just to tell his mother he was living near the beach. After a few months of naked bliss, he got a letter from her saying, "Dear Son, as I have no recent photos of you, can you please send me the most recent one you have? Love, Mom."

Well, the man didn't have any photos of himself that didn't show him naked, so he decided to chop one in half and send just the top half. A few weeks later, he got a letter from his mother saying, "Thanks for the photo, and could you send another to your grandma?" And so he did, but he made a mistake and sent her the wrong half. The man got really upset but then remembered his grandmother's poor eyesight, and he decided it would be okay.

Two weeks later, he gets a letter back from her saying: "Dear Grandson, I think your photo is great. But you really should change your hairstyle—it makes your nose look too big."

Mr. Adams had been retired for a year when his wife of fifty years suggested they take a cruise: "We could go somewhere for a week, and make wild love like we did when we were young!" He quickly agreed.

He put on his hat and went down to the pharmacy, where he bought a bottle of motion-sickness pills and a box of condoms. Upon returning home, his wife said, "I've been thinking. There is no reason we can't go for a month."

So Mr. Adams went back to the pharmacy and asked for three more bottles of motion-sickness pills and a box of condoms. When he returned his wife said, "You know, since the children are all grown up, what's stopping us from cruising the world?"

So back to the pharmacy he went, and carried 48 bottles of motion-sickness pills and the same number of condoms up to the counter. The pharmacist finally got curious. "You know, Mr. Adams, you have been doing business with me for over thirty years. I certainly don't mean to pry, but if it makes you that sick, why the hell do you do it?"

A little boy walked in on his parents having sex and asked what they were doing. His father replied, "Well, you know how you've always wanted a little brother? That's what I'm doing—I'm putting a little brother in Mommy for you." The little boy nodded and went back to bed.

The next day the father came home from work and the little boy was on the front porch crying. When his father asked what was wrong, he replied, "You know how you put a baby in my mommy last night? The mailman came to the house this morning and ate him!"

<hr />

Q: WHAT DOES A WOMAN DO WITH HER ASSHOLE BEFORE HAVING REALLY GOOD SEX?

A: She drops him off at the golf course on her way to the bar.

<hr />

A Men's Glossary (Part II):

"Haven't I seen you before?" = You have a nice ass.

"I need you." = My hand is tired.

"I really want to get to know you better." = So I can tell my friends about having sex with you.

"I've been thinking a lot." = You're not as attractive as when I was drunk.

<hr />

Q: WHAT IS THE DIFFERENCE BETWEEN "OOOOH!" AND "AAAAH!"?

A: About three inches.

<hr />

This guy walks into a bar down in Mississippi and orders a mudslide. The bartender looks at the man and says, "You're not from 'round here, are ya?"

"No," replies the man, "I'm from Pennsylvania."

The bartender looks at him and says, "Well, what do you do in Pennsylvania?"

"I'm a taxidermist," says the man.

The bartender, looking very bewildered, now asks, "What in the world is a tax-e-derm-ist?"

The man looks at the bartender and says, "Well, I mount dead animals."

The bartender stands back and hollers to the whole barful of guys who are staring at him, "It's okay, boys! He's one of us!"

***

Q: HOW CAN YOU TELL WHO THE BLIND MAN IS IN A NUD-IST COLONY?
A: It isn't hard.

***

Married men should forget about their faults and their mistakes. There's no need for two people to remember the same things.

***

A large, powerfully built guy named Bruce meets a woman named Cindy at a bar. After a number of drinks, they agree to go back to his place. As they are making out in the bedroom, Bruce stands up and starts to undress. After he takes his shirt off, he flexes his muscular arms and says, "See that, baby? That's 1,000 pounds of dynamite!" Cindy begins to drool.

Bruce then drops his pants, strikes a bodybuilder's pose, and says, referring to his bulging thighs, "See those, baby? That's 1,000 pounds of dynamite!" Cindy is just aching for action at this point.

Finally, Bruce drops his underpants, and after a quick glance, Cindy grabs her purse and runs screaming to the front door. Bruce catches her before she is able to leave and asks, "Why are you in such a hurry to go?"

Cindy replies, "With 2,000 pounds of dynamite and such a short fuse, I was afraid you were about to blow!"

John has his mother over for dinner in his apartment with his female roommate. His mother has long been suspected a romantic link between the two, but John has just as long denied it. During dinner, watching them interact, she becomes more convinced than before. While the roommate is washing the dishes, the mother presses again, but John tells her absolutely nothing is going on, and that he is not living in sin.

Four days later, the roommate asks John if his mother has a problem with stealing. It seems that the sterling-silver corkscrew is missing.

John doubts that his mother is a thief, but agrees to write a letter anyway. "Mom: I'm not saying you did steal it, and I'm not saying you didn't steal it, but the fact is the corkscrew is missing."

Two days later, he receives a letter back: "Dear Johnny, I'm not saying you are sleeping with your roommate, and I'm not saying you're not, but the fact is, if she were sleeping in her own bed, she would have found the corkscrew by now."

Q: WHAT ARE SNOWBALLS?

A: The difference between a snowman and a snowv

Q: WHY DID THE BALD MAN TEAR HOLES IN HIS PANTS POCKETS?

A: So he could run his hands through his hair.

During the wedding rehearsal, the groom approached the pastor with an unusual offer.

"Look, I'll give you $500 if you'll change the wedding vows. When you get to the part where I'm to promise to 'love, honor, and obey,' I'd appreciate it if you'd just leave it out." He passed the minister five Benjamin Franklins and walked away satisfied.

The day of the wedding, the pastor begins his made-to-order vows: "Will you promise to prostrate yourself before her, obey her every command and wish, serve her breakfast in bed every morning of your life, and swear eternally before God and your lovely wife that you will not ever even look at another woman, as long as you both shall live?"

The groom gulps, looks around, and says in a tiny voice, "Yes." Then he leans toward the pastor and hisses: "I thought we had a deal."

The pastor puts the $500 into the groom's hand and whispers: "She made me a better offer."

Q: WHAT'S THE FASTEST WAY TO A MAN'S HEART?

A: Through his chest with a sharp knife.

Little Johnny walked into his dad's bedroom one day only to catch him sitting on the side of his bed sliding on a condom. Johnny's father, in an attempt to hide his full erection with a condom on it, bent over as if to look under the bed. Little Johnny asked curiously, "What ya doin,' Dad?"

His father quickly replied, "I thought I saw a rat go underneath the bed."

"Really," Johnny asked. "Can you see him?"

"No, not yet," the father said, still straining to hide his package.

"What are you gonna do if you catch him?" Johnny asked. "Fuck him?"

Q: HOW CAN YOU TELL WHEN YOU HUSBAND IS DEAD?
A: You get the same amount of sex, but football is never on.

A woman was having an affair during the day while her husband was at work. One day she heard his car pull into the driveway. She yelled to her boyfriend, "Hurry! Grab your clothes and jump out the window; my husband's home early!"

The boyfriend looked out the window and said, "But it's raining cats and dogs out there!"

She said, "If my husband catches us in here, he'll kill us both!" So the boyfriend grabbed his clothes and jumped out the window.

As he began running down the street, he discovered he'd run right into the middle of a town marathon, so he ran along beside the others. Still naked, his clothes tucked under his arm, he tried to blend in as best he could.

One of the runners asked him, "Do you always run in the nude?"

He answered, while gasping for air, "Oh yes, it feels so free having the air blow over your skin while you run."

The other runner then asked the nude man, "Do you always run carrying your clothes under your arm?"

The nude man answered breathlessly, "Oh yes, that way I can get dressed right at the end of the run for the drive home."

The runner then asked, "Do you always wear a condom when you run?"

The nude man replied, "Only if it's raining."

🙂

Q: WHY IS SLEEPING WITH A MAN LIKE A SOAP OPERA?
A: Just when it gets interesting, they're done until next time.

🙂

This woman goes into a dentist's office. After he is through examining her, he says, "I am sorry to tell you this, but I am going to have to drill a tooth."

The woman says, "Oooooh, the pain is so awful, I'd rather have a baby!"

The dentist replies, "Make up your mind. I have to adjust the chair."

🙂

A retired gentlemen went into the Social Security office to apply for Social Security.

After waiting in line a long time, he got to the counter. The woman behind the counter asked him for his driver's license to verify his age. He looked in his pockets and realized he had left his wallet at home. He told the woman that he was very sorry but he seemed to have left his wallet at home. "Will I have to go home and come back now?" he asks. The woman says, "Unbutton your shirt."

So he opens his shirt, revealing lots of curly silver hair.

She says, "That silver hair on your chest is proof enough for me," and she processes his application. When he gets home, the man excitedly tells his wife about his experience at the Social Security office.

His wife says, "You should have dropped your pants; you might have qualified for disability, too."

A man goes to an emergency room with a blue testicle.

"This is very serious," the physician says. "We'll have to amputate or you'll die."

"Oh, I was afraid of that," the man says. "But go ahead."

The next morning, the man is back again. This time, his other testicle and his penis are blue.

"Good Lord," the doctor says. "It's spreading." And he amputates his other testicle and his penis, and inserts a plastic tube for urinating.

That night, the man is back. "Doc, now the plastic tube has turned blue!"

"Really?" the doctor says. He looks pensive for a moment. "Maybe your jeans are bleeding dye."

Q: WHAT'S THE DEFINITION OF A BACHELOR?
A: A selfish asshole depriving some woman of her right to alimony.

Q: WHAT'S THE MAIN DIFFERENCE BETWEEN AN ORAL A RECTAL THERMOMETER?

A: The taste.

At dinner, a husband tells his wife: "I'm going to try a new position tonight: me lying back with my hands behind my head, getting a blow job."

"What's new about that?" his wife asks.

"I'll be at a massage parlor downtown."

A college professor was reviewing for the final exam with his class and stressed that there would no excuses for missing it, except a severe medical problem, such as heart failure or brain seizure.

"What about extreme sexual exhaustion?" a smart-ass yelled from his seat in the back.

"In that case, you'll have to write with your other hand, Mr. Reilly," the professor answered.

Q: WHAT'S THE DIFFERENCE BETWEEN A BOYFRIEND AND A HUSBAND?

A: Forty-five minutes.

A guy is riding the bus when the most beautiful woman he has ever seen gets on. The only problem is that she is a nun. He decides to approach her anyway. "Sister, you are the most beautiful woman I've ever seen and I must have sex with you," he says.

"I'm sorry but I've given my body to God," she replies, and then gets off the bus at the next stop.

Suddenly the bus driver turns around to the guy and says, "I know a way you can get her in the sack." He tells the guy about how the nun goes to confession every day at 3:00 P.M. He tells the guy his plan and the guy leaves happy, knowing he's going to get some.

The next day at three, the guy is in the booth dressed as a priest. When the nun approaches in the darkness, he says, "Sister, God has told me I must have sex with you."

She replies, "Well, if God has said it, we must do it. However, because of my strong commitment to God, I will only take it up the ass."

The guy figures this isn't a problem and proceeds to have great sex with her. After it is over, he whips off his cassock and says, "Surprise—I'm the guy on the bus."

With that, the nun whips off her habit and says, "Surprise—I'm the bus driver."

A high-school English teacher assigned his class a composition about the house in which each of them lived. One boy got his back with an F. The teacher explained it was because it was the same essay his older brother had handed in the previous year.

"Of course it is," the boy said. "It's the same house."

Two jocks are driving down the freeway chugging a few beers when they see a roadblock ahead with police checking for drunk drivers. The jock in the passenger seat starts to panic,

but the driver tells him to calm down and do what he do
then quickly chugs the last of the beer in his hand, pee
label off, sticks the bottle under the seat, and presses the label
to his forehead. The second jock follows along. When they arrive at the roadblock, a police officer looks in and is quite surprised by this spectacle.

The cop says, "Hello, gentlemen. By any chance, have you
two been drinking tonight?"

"Why no, Officer," the driver says. "You see, we're on the
patch!"

<hr>

Q: HOW MANY REDNECKS DOES IT TAKE TO SCREW IN A LIGHT-
BULB?
A: Fuck it. We'll just drink in the dark.

<hr>

A married man was talking to his buddy, and he said, "I don't
know what to get my wife for her birthday. She has *everything,* and besides, she can afford to buy anything she wants,
so I'm stumped."

His buddy said, "I have an idea. Why don't you make up a
certificate saying she can have sixty minutes of great sex, any
way she wants it? She'll probably be thrilled."

So the fellow did just that. The next day his buddy said,
"Well? Did you take my suggestion?"

"Yes, I did," said the fellow.

"Did she like it?" his buddy asked.

"Yep. She jumped up, thanked me, kissed me on the forehead, and ran out the door, yelling, 'I'll be back in an hour!'"

<hr>

A man decided to paint the toilet while his wife was on a business trip. His wife came home sooner than he expected, used the toilet, and got her rear stuck to the seat. She was so upset, she asked her husband to drive her to the doctor. She put a large overcoat on to cover the seat before they went. When they got to the doctor's office, the man lifted his wife's coat to show him the problem.

The man asked, "Doctor, have you ever seen anything like this before?"

"Sure," the doctor replied, "but never framed."

***

Q: HOW MANY REAL MEN DOES IT TAKE TO SCREW IN A LIGHTBULB?
A: None. Real Men aren't afraid of the dark.

***

Q: WHY DO ONLY 10 PERCENT OF MEN MAKE IT TO HEAVEN?
A: Because if they all went, it would be Hell.

***

Q: HOW IS A MAN LIKE A SNOWSTORM?
A: You don't know when it's going to come, how many inches you'll get, or how long it will last.

***

A golfer was having a long, long game and turned his rage on his young caddy. "You're terrible!" he screamed. "When we get back to the clubhouse, I'm going to get you fired!"

"That's okay by me," the caddy replied. "By the time we

get back to the clubhouse, I'll be old enough to get a regular job."

Q: WHAT'S THE DIFFERENCE BETWEEN A PORCUPINE AND A CORVETTE?
A: The porcupine has pricks on the outside.

Good advice for a new groom: Never argue with your wife when she's tired. Or rested.

Q: WHY DON'T MEN NAME THEIR PENISES AFTER WOMEN?
A: They don't want women running their lives.

You might be married to a redneck if he's always wondering how gas stations keep their bathrooms so clean.

Losing a husband can be hard. In many women's cases, it's damn near impossible.

Two women who were having lunch together began discussing cosmetic surgery.

The first woman says, "I'll be honest with you, I'm getting a boob job."

The second woman says, "Oh, that's nothing. I'm thinking of having my asshole bleached."

To which the first replies, "Wow! All of him, or just his hair?"

Q: WHAT DO YOU CALL A MAN WITH HALF A BRAIN?
A: Gifted.

Q: WHAT DO ELECTRIC TOY TRAINS AND BREASTS HAVE IN COMMON?
A: They're made for children, but it's the husbands who end up playing with them.

A traveling salesman was testifying in his divorce trial about his wife's alleged infidelity. "Mr. Hanes, what makes you think my client was cheating on you?" his wife's lawyer asked.

"Well, I was never home during the week for five straight months," the man began. "When I got home that weekend, my wife and I were in the middle of a pretty ferocious lovemaking session when the landlady started pounding on her ceiling. She yelled: 'Can't you at least cut that out on the weekends?'"

Behind every great woman is a man telling her she's ignoring him.

Some women are gathered and the subject of conversation turns to sex and then birth control.

The first woman says, "We're Catholic, so we can't use it."

The next woman says, "I am, too, but we use the rhythm method."

The third woman says, "We use the bucket-and-saucer method."

"What the heck is the bucket-and-saucer method?" the others ask.

"Well, I'm five foot eleven and my husband is five foot two. We make love standing up with him standing on a bucket, and when his eyes get big as saucers, I kick the bucket out from under him."

Q: WHAT DO MEN AND APES HAVE IN COMMON?
A: Are you serious?

Q: HOW IS A BATTERY DIFFERENT FROM A MAN?
A: A battery has a positive side.

Q: WHAT DO MOST MARRIED MEN FANTASIZE WHEN HAVING SEX WITH THEIR WIVES?
A: That their wives aren't fantasizing.

Grandpa and Grandma were living with their son and daughter-in-law. Grandpa noticed his son's bottle of Viagra in the medicine cabinet and asked if he could have one.

"Well, Dad, they're kind of expensive. They cost ten dollars each."

"That's okay, son. I just want one, and I'll pay for it."

Grandpa only had a fifty-dollar bill, so he said he'd leave the money under his son's pillow later that night.

The next morning, his son found $110 under his pillow, and he said to his father, "Dad, I told you it was only $10. You left me $110!"

"I know, son," Grandpa said. "The other hundred is from Grandma."